Career Launcher

Performing Arts

Celia Watson Seupel

Checkmark Books®
An imprint of Infobase Publishing

Career Launcher: **Performing Arts**

Checkmark Books
An imprint of Infobase Publishing
132 West 31st Street
New York NY 10001

Library of Congress Cataloging-in-Publication Data

Seupel, Celia W.
    Performing arts / Celia Watson Seupel ; foreword by Teresa Eyring.
        p. cm. — (Career launcher)
    Includes bibliographical references and index.
    ISBN-13: 978-0-8160-7953-7 (hardcover : alk. paper)
    ISBN-10: 0-8160-7953-6 (hardcover : alk. paper)
    ISBN-13: 978-0-8160-7975-9 (pbk. : alk. paper)
    ISBN-10: 0-8160-7975-7 (pbk. : alk. paper)
1. Performing arts—Vocational guidance—Juvenile literature. I. Title.
    PN1580.S48 2010
    791.023—dc22

                                                          2009049370

Checkmark Books are available at special discounts when purchased in bulk quantities for businesses, associations, institutions, or sales promotions. Please call our Special Sales Department in New York at (212) 967-8800 or (800) 322-8755.

You can find Ferguson on the World Wide Web at (http://www.fergpubco.com

Produced by Print Matters, Inc.
Text design by A Good Thing, Inc.
Cover design by Takeshi Takahashi
Cover printed by Art Print Company, Taylor, PA
Book printed and bound by Maple Press, York, PA
Dated printed: August 2010

Printed in the United States of America

10 9 8 7 6 5 4 3 2 1

This book is printed on acid-free paper.

Contents

Foreword

I believe in the arts. I believe the arts have an important impact on how people view the world. When I was starting out—I had just graduated from college and I was working for the Wooly Mammoth Theatre—my job seemed very marginalized. That has changed dramatically in the last 25 years. Today, theater and the performing arts are much more accepted as part of our society. Performing arts management is a legitimate career option.

The field has grown dramatically since the 1960s. Since then, the handful of theaters across the country has grown to number about 2,000. At Theatre Communications Group, our original 1960s membership swelled from 10 or 12 theaters to 500 members today. The 1960s is when it all blossomed—the dawn of the regional theater movement. And that is just theater! Other performing arts boomed as well: dance, music, presenting, opera...not to mention the many nonprofit organizations that support the performing arts.

Up until recently, there were many job opportunities. Right now, it is tougher: Most nonprofits are cutting staff and budgets.

No matter what the state of the economy, a good place to begin is in the field of development. Fund-raising is a great way to get a foot in the door, and often there are not as many qualified applicants for fund-raising positions. As a performing arts manager, fund-raising experience will give you a skill you can use for the rest of your career. The skill is helpful even in the commercial sector, where you have to find investors. You learn how to make a case for your project. Typically, people think they are not going to like fund-raising; they think that it is all about asking for money. In fact, it is all about relationships. It is a process of building relationships and articulating a case for something you are passionate about. A really talented fund-raiser is sought after and may even be lured away by the higher wages in the hospital or university world. In the end, though, if you are in the arts, it is because you love it and want to be around it, not because of the size of your salary.

The newcomer to the field might want to think about his or her ultimate goal. I have colleagues who started out working in the box office and are now managing directors. Even though that still can happen in a smaller organization, it does not seem to happen very much anymore. If your goal is to be an executive director, it is important to understand *all* aspects of running an organization: finances, marketing, development, and human resources. Again, fund-raising is important: Lack of fund-raising experience can be an obstacle to advancement. You learn critical skills through fund-raising. For example, when you put together grants, you learn how to work with a board; you learn about human resources, bargaining with unions, and budgets. The trend is to expect the executive director to do more fund-raising than she or he did 25 years ago. A good fund-raiser thinks strategically, from the institution's point of view. Graduate school is important, but there are certain things you cannot learn from school. You need to know the nuts and bolts, plus wisdom from being in the hot seat!

When I was starting my career, one of the things I did right by accident was to focus. In graduate school (Yale), I focused on theater. Although in performing arts we collaborate across theater, dance, and the other arts, there are big differences among them in business as well as artistically. For example, if you have been a public relations specialist for an orchestra, it will be easier for you to move on to director of public relations in the music world rather than in theater. It is an advantage to focus on one area.

Mentors have been crucial for me. I had great advisors. In fact, in my first job at Wooly Mammoth, I worked for Howard Shalwitz, who built that organization. He was an extraordinary artist and thinker, and my first mentor. It was while I was working and learning from Howard that I realized I was interested in arts management, not just fund-raising.

Mentors are an important source of help as you advance your career. There are different ways people connect with such an advisor. You might happen upon someone who is very knowledgeable at school, or it might be someone you have interned with. You might even ask to interview someone you respect. So often, people are willing to help. You might just ask: "Can you give me a little time to help me think about my career objectives?"

In my career, I have been lucky to work with some of the best artists and visionaries. When your job is to support the artistic vision of an artist or an organization, you need to be enormously excited by whomever you are supporting. That is why it is important to take time every day to become more knowledgeable about the arts generally. Who are the artists internationally? Who is doing what? Do your research before you interview. Know the organization's mission, its programming, its key players. Know who you want to work for, and understand your own standards. Make sure, whatever you do, that it is your passion.

—Teresa Eyring, Executive Director
THEATRE COMMUNICATIONS GROUP,
NEW YORK, NEW YORK

Acknowledgments

So many people helped me understand the world of performing arts and gave unselfishly of their time, it is impossible to thank them all individually. A special word of thanks goes out to all of my interviewees, who not only graciously took time out of busy schedules to talk to a writer completely unknown to them, but who also were willing to answer many follow up questions. Thanks to Michael M. Kaiser for allowing me to quote part of his blog, and to the relatives of Fann Taylor for allowing me to reproduce her interesting memo from the early days of performing arts management education. Thanks to Teresa Eyring for generously consenting to allow me to use her wonderful and open interview as the foreword for this book. Also I am grateful to Professors Andrew Taylor and Brann Wry, who extended themselves to be helpful to me and to this project, and to Professors Arthur Dirks, Wayne Turney, and Walter Englert, who helped explain some of American theater history. Special thanks to singer and songwriter, Ellie Sartie, who helped me create the *Resources and Talk Like A Pro* chapters when I was lagging seriously behind deadline.

Introduction

Exploring the world of the performing arts and management is like opening the door onto an unexpected and delightful garden. It is a field of endeavor populated by very creative and passionate people who help to make the world a more beautiful place. These are people who love the performing arts; people who are often musicians, actors, or dancers themselves; people who give unstintingly to help bring performers and audiences together in new and successful ways. If you are passionate about live performing arts—music, opera, dance, and theater—and would like to be a part of that world; if you enjoy the art of business and have a desire to bring audiences together with performers or to promote the nature of the artistic experience, then performing arts management may be for you.

Rather than reviewing the field of live performing arts academically, this book is a seat-of-the-pants guide. It is meant to help the beginning professional get his or her bearings and go on to do well. For example, the book's many interviews with successful performing arts professionals will give you great insider information about how to succeed on the job. Just reading each interviewee's bio gives insight into how performing arts careers grow and change.

You can read this book straight through from beginning to end, or you can take it piecemeal, choosing chapters according to your interest. Chapter One, the history of the performing arts in the United States, in an entertaining story unto itself, especially the early years of struggle amongst our stern Puritan forebears. Find out why theaters were so sinful in the old days (sometimes they really were). Who were the brave pioneer performers that cracked the forbidding frontier of American performing arts, eventually bringing respectability? Read about how creative enterprise became stifled by the first performing arts monopoly. And discover how the world of the performing arts—at one time a purely for-profit business—split apart into nonprofit artistic enterprise and for-profit commercial entertainment.

This split deserves a separate comment. Technology, from movies and TV to the Internet, has increasingly edged out the commercial viability of live performance. Not only have the recorded performing arts become spectacularly popular, they can produce more income per dollar spent, inviting greater investment than live performance. In theater, with few exceptions, only Broadway remains commercially competitive—and Broadway is struggling. Dance, as an art form unto itself, is rarely commercially viable in today's world. To support a dance troupe with salaries, health insurance, rehearsal space, advertising, and performance space has become a prohibitive expense, too expensive to rely upon an income of ticket receipts alone.

Music does compete in the for-profit, commercial sector (think screaming fans and crowded stadiums), but live music performance is inextricably integrated with the recording industry (CDs, TV, movies, and Internet presence), creating a synergistic income for those performances. Classical music and opera, needless to say, do not compete in the same arena. The for-profit and nonprofit industries of live performing arts diverge at the bottom line. Leaders in the commercial sector are guided by promoting what will sell; leaders in the nonprofit sector are guided by artistic excellence. This divergence, together with public support of nonprofits, has created two very different worlds in the performing arts, managed in two different ways.

On the other hand, an interesting development in economic hard times is the pressure for nonprofits to behave a little bit more like commercial enterprises. There is a current movement for nonprofits to reconsider the for-profit model, and for the artistic motivation to make room for a little commercial enterprise. Trends in opera, for example (see Chapter Two, "State of the Industry"), show an increasing reliance on the more popular standards, with reduced production of new and innovative music. Classical orchestras are inviting pop singers to perform highly saleable shows wedged in between shows from their more traditional repertoire.

Chapter Two also examines some difficult questions in the world of the performing arts. A seminal study in the 1960s by Baumol and Bowen demonstrated that, given the inevitable expense, the live performing arts can *never* be self-sustaining by earned income alone. The study gave rise, in those flush times, to new and more dedicated public foundations and funding for the arts: The National Foundation for the Arts, regional and state arts counsels, and private foundation commitments. Today, however, the temperature of the American cultural climate has been trending toward the decidedly cold. Philanthropists and taxpayers alike are becoming increasingly skeptical of art as a social good, and performing arts organizations are looking toward maximizing profits without sacrificing artistic excellence. Meanwhile, the for-profit sector is turning increasingly toward digital dollars, maximizing return on investment with technology that excludes the onstage experience.

In Chapter Three, "On the Job," you will find an A to Z listing of the many jobs that go into creating the performing arts environment. These are people who decide on the artistic direction for a theater and the people who do the fund-raising to make it happen; the people who take care of the sets and the floors, the people who take the tickets, and the people who go out into the community and make sure the audience knows where and when to come. This chapter helps you not only see how many jobs there are and how each one contributes to the performing arts, but also helps you to see how your particular job fits into the whole scene.

To succeed at any job takes a combination of luck, knowledge, and (most importantly) hard work. But hard work will not get the job done if you do not know where to focus, and luck comes to those who put themselves in the right place at the right time. Chapter Four, "Tips for Success," goes into the details of how to do just that. While every interview in this book is loaded with tips for success, this particular chapter gives you the low-down on how to succeed in the performing arts. Specifically, how to make the most of any job you get, how to network, and how to find a mentor are perhaps the three most important tools for doing a good job and advancing your career.

Perhaps nothing makes a person feel greener on the job than misunderstanding jargon. While you may not mistake "merge-purge" for a new kind of bulimia, you might find yourself confusing a "dry tech" with a very boring technical rehearsal—when, in fact, it means a technical rehearsal without actors. (And, with or without actors, *all* technical rehearsals are boring.) Chapter Five, "Talk Like a Pro," will introduce you to some of the vocabulary that goes along with the job. This glossary is a mixture of music, dance, theater, fund-raising, and business. To understand it is to understand the inside of the industry itself, and, while some words will be familiar, reading through the jargon may introduce some concepts you will stumble upon whatever your particular field of endeavor.

If anything abounds in the field of performing arts—besides talent, of course—it is resources. Not necessarily the kind of resources with dollar signs attached, but very much the kind that offers professional help, solidarity, networking, caring, and commitment. Chapter Six, "Resources," gives you a list of where to turn whether you need questions answered or a whole new field explained. Professional associations and organizations exist for almost every field of endeavor. The conferences listed here are terrific places to network and learn about the latest developments in your field. And if you are thinking about graduate school, the universities and programs included in this chapter are among the very best.

It is hoped that you will find this book useful, interesting, and practical. The advice comes straight from the folks who have started at the bottom and worked their way up. The tips and resources in this book should give you a place from which to step forward into your career with confidence.

Chapter 1

Industry History

Who was the first performing arts manager? Probably, it was the *archon eponymous* of ancient Athens, 6th century B.C.E. It was up to this public official to select three poets (out of the many deserving and talented writers who submitted excellent proposals) who would get to produce their plays for the Greater Dionysia festival competition. The archon also selected the patrons, or the *choregos*. The production was publicly funded by a tax on the wealthy and each wealthy *choregos* gave his tax money directly to a chosen poet. The archon was responsible for selecting actors for the plays and for putting together a panel of judges to award first, second, and third prizes to the poets. The prize, if the poets were lucky, might be a goat! Today, we call these people grant administrators and they tend to work for nonprofit corporations. The basic idea, however, remains the same: People who love the arts help performers give pleasure, beauty, enrichment, and entertainment to audiences.

Fast Facts

Renaissance Arts Integration

Contemporary arts integration may have begun with the Italian Renaissance, which combined the arts of theater, dance, and music with food. Consider, for example, the Italian Court's 1489 presentation of *Jason and the Golden Fleece*, dramatized with music and dance just before the roast lamb was served.

There have always been behind-the-scenes managers in the performing arts, people who bring productions together and enable the show to carry on. After the Classical period and Western civilization's decline into the Dark Ages when only morality plays managed by the clergy were permitted, the performing arts reemerged during the Italian Renaissance, especially as musical and dance entertainment for the wealthy.

The Elizabethan Era: 1500–1600

In the early days of England, just before the Elizabethan era, traveling troupes of performers gathered audiences and pennies in the public town squares. English innkeepers, with their capacious cobblestone courtyards, recognized a business opportunity when they saw one. They hosted traveling troupes at their inns and organized performances in their courtyards, where large crowds could gather into proper audiences. Most importantly, each member of the audience would have to pay to get into the courtyard to see the show. For the performers, this worked better than relying on the goodwill of those who gathered in the public square. The practice enriched both the performers and the innkeepers. Theater and theater management were born.

The first real European theater as we know it was simply called "The Theatre" and was built in 1576 in Shoreditch, London, by James Burbage. About 23 years later, Shakespeare's Globe Theatre was built. James Burbage, an actor himself as well as a theatrical entrepreneur, is credited with giving the young Shakespeare his start; Burbage's son Richard was one of Shakespeare's leading actors.

Performing Arts in Colonial America: 1650–1800

The performing arts had a rocky start in the American colonies, thanks to Puritan mores of the day. Such frivolities and entertainments were believed to have the power to corrupt the young and to lead their elders into sin. For New England colonists in particular, "the playhouse" was not only immoral, but also illegal.

According to historian Arthur Hornblow, amateur actors in the colonies were summoned to court in 1665 after committing the grave sin of performing in public. Of all the American colonies, Hornblow relates that only Virginia and Maryland did not prohibit "playacting" by law. These more southern colonies and, increasingly, cosmopolitan residents of larger cities, were closer to mother England and her felonious pleasures. The lure of drama, in any case, was not to be denied; the history of the era's legislation shows that the letter of the law was repeatedly tested and ignored. There can be no doubt that performances took place in the colonies, since stringent objections and legal impediments sought to deter them.

In perhaps the first play written by an American and acted in America, Harvard students performed Benjamin Colman's *Gustavus Vasa* in 1690. Noted English actor Anthony Aston (aka "Mat Medley"), reported acting in New York City in 1702 or thereabout. According to Hornblow, a 1714 letter by Justice Samuel Sewall objects to the calumny of a play to be performed in the Council Chamber of Boston, writing, "Lct not Christian Boston goe beyond Heathen Rome in the practice of Shamefull vanities." The play's venue was changed.

Not only were dance and music a part of theatrical performances, ballet companies toured the colonies as well. As early as 1735, England's Henry Holt and his group performed three ballets in Charleston, South Carolina. Also in Charleston, dancers Alexander Placide and his wife performed a ballet in 1791. A year later, they were joined by George Washington's favorite performer and America's first professional dancer, John Durang, for a season in New York City.

Performing Arts Management in Colonial Times

The story of the performing arts and its management is entwined with the history of the theaters themselves. While performers have always created their own troupes and companies—often serving as manager, administrator, and lead performer, too—it is in the work of owners and managers of theaters that we see the beginnings of the modern vocation of performing arts management.

During the Colonial period, the first permanent theater spaces in America were established. In 1732, a theater opened in New York City consisting of the second floor of a building with seating for about 400. Another theater, the Playhouse on Dock Street, opened in 1736 in Charleston, South Carolina. Thomas Kean, a famous English actor, performed *Richard III* at New York's two-storied First Nassau Street Theatre in March of 1750.

Predating all of these, however, was a theater built in Williamsburg, Virginia, in 1716, by one of the first American performing arts managers. According to Williamsburg historian Lyon Tyler, a merchant named William Levingston was the manager of a traveling dance school and also managed the school's lead dancers, Charles and Mary Stagg. A 1716 contract between Levingston and the Staggs states that Levingston would build a theater and provide actors, sets, and music from England. Levingston, good to his word, bought three and a half acres in Williamsburg and built a residence as well as a theater and a bowling alley. Unfortunately, the theater did not flourish for long; its mortgage was foreclosed in 1723, and eventually the building was turned into a Town Hall.

Despite the appearance of playhouses in the colonies, many leaders were still busy fighting the trend. In 1750, so many people flocked to see a production of Thomas Otway's *The Orphan* at a Boston coffeehouse (performed by local amateurs and two English professionals), a riot broke out on the street. As a result, the General Court banished acting from the Commonwealth and made it a criminal offense, punishable by a fine, to even attend a performance.

On the Cutting Edge

Evolutions in Lighting

Edison's incandescent light bulb in 1879 makes the use of electricity feasible. Theatrical lighting with electricity begins about 1885, eliminating the considerable danger due to gas lighting fires, which were common at this time. By 1900, nearly every major theater uses electric lights.

According to Hornblow, the state of Pennsylvania passed laws prohibiting plays in 1759, promising a penalty of 500 pounds for offenders; Rhode Island followed suit in 1761. In 1762, the New Hampshire House of Representatives, which would not allow an acting troupe into Portsmouth, stated that plays had a "peculiar influence on the minds of young people and greatly endanger their morals by giving them a taste for intriguing, amusement and pleasure."

Opposition to theater was not as unreasonable as it sounds today. In Europe, and later in America, prostitution was practiced openly in the upper galleries of theaters; drinking and general riotousness of the audience as well as crowds that milled about outside the theater furthered the ill repute of the performing arts.

Theatrical managers (usually actors as well as managers of their own companies) struggled hard to redeem the performing arts in the public eye. One such actor and manager was Lewis Hallem.

Although a fine English actor, Hallem was apparently more interested in the family business of managing a performance company, and often cast others in choice roles. Hallem first arrived in New York around 1750 with his talented actress wife. Armed with testimonials from England to assure local magistrates of his company's good character, he was nevertheless denied permission to perform. In 1752, The Hallems went to Williamsburg, Virginia, to seek a more welcoming climate. Upon returning to New York in 1753, Hallem appealed to the public by written petition to be allowed to perform, and was finally granted permission to work in New York. Hallem produced at least 21 plays between September 17, 1753, to March 18, 1754, in a theater he built on Nassau Street to replace the original, smaller theater. A good manager, he evidently made enough money to pay his bills: before moving on to Philadelphia, he publicly announced that his creditors should come and collect whatever he owed to them.

Sadly, Lewis Hallem died in 1758, and the gifted Mrs. Hallem married David Douglass, who took over the company as manager. More of a talented manager than actor, Douglass became an important producer, building the successful Theatre on John Street in New York in 1767 (where decades later George Washington himself attended a play), until the revolution put an end to his work in America.

The Performing Arts after the American Revolution

With the American Revolution, the status of the performing arts again took a dive. The Continental Congress passed a resolution in 1776 that frowned upon playhouse "entertainments," prompting even more states to pass legislation that outlawed stage performance.

Amusement and pleasure, nevertheless, had its way: In the 1780s and 1790s, these laws were repealed, and the performing arts flourished. In New York City, enthusiastic audiences prompted eleven wealthy New Yorkers, at the cost of $375 per share, to build a celebrated world class theater on Chatham Street (later Park Row) called the Park Theatre. The project, designed by famous French architect Marc Isambard Brunel (who had fled to New York from France's reign of terror), ran over budget.

After raising what amounted to more than $130,000, the theater opened under the management of the Hallem's son, Lewis Hallem "the Younger," who had taken over his parents' performance company and was known as a fine and successful actor (but a rather temperamental and poor manager) and John Hodgkinson. Despite society's ebullient greeting of the new and lavish theater when it finally opened on January 27, 1798, keeping the theater afloat financially was a problem. Hallem and Hodgkinson left soon after the theater opened, and a third partner, William Dunlap, tried to make a go of it. He did not succeed, declaring bankruptcy in 1805; evidently, his expenses were so great, he would have had to make at least $1,200 a week to break even. The theater was sold to John Jacob Astor and John Beekman. Under the management of Stephen Price and Edmund Simpson, the theater became more profitable. Price and Simpson imported English stars and actors, which appealed to New York society, and the neighborhood around the theater had improved. From about 1810 to 1830, it was the place to go and be seen.

Developing American Performing Arts: 1800–1900

Dance was a vaunted pastime for the aristocratic European courts, and so its reputation in Puritan America languished along with other "decadent" theatrical presentations. Nevertheless, by the midnineteenth century, there were up and coming ballet stars who studied at Mme. and M. Paul Hazard's ballet academy in Philadelphia: Augusta Maywood, who became famous in Europe, and Mary Ann Lee, who toured America in the 1840s. With the introduction of the Russian Ballet to America in the early twentieth century and with the development of modern dance, dance became a major and respected art form in America.

The symphony also gained a foothold in America after the Revolution. Harvard claims to have the oldest American symphony orchestra, dating its Harvard College Orchestra (now the Harvard-Radcliffe Orchestra) back to 1809. It was formed originally by six Harvard students who called themselves the "Pierian Sodality." The Sodality was a fellowship devoted to the nine Muses of ancient Grecian Mount Pieria, and seemed especially to embody Alexander Pope's dictum, "Drink deep, or taste not the Pierian Spring," since their regular activities included not only playing instruments and singing but also drinking, carousing, and serenading beautiful women. By 1908, the Sodality had become a serious musical organization, performing as the Harvard University Orchestra. The Sodality's Centennial Tour through the state of New York was very popular. As the orchestra began to tour the country, it built a national reputation.

The New York Philharmonic claims to be the oldest professional American symphony orchestra still in existence. Its evolution demonstrates the value of good management. The orchestra was founded in 1842 by American-born Ureli Corelli Hill, a violinist who was also the conductor for his group of local musicians. The cooperative performed successfully under a variety of leaderships until 1902, when two society women of the time, Mary Seney Sheldon and Minnie Untermyer, led a group of wealthy New Yorkers who organized to support the orchestra. The musicians' cooperative then became a corporation. Under this new and more liberating structure—in which Gustav Mahler, a legendary composer, was brought in to be principal conductor—performances were increased from 18 per year to 54, opera was eliminated from the program in favor of symphonic music (a first for a symphony orchestra), and musicians' salaries were guaranteed.

The Tour in Post–Civil War America

The Civil War (1860–65) wrought a great change in American performing arts. According to theater professor Arthur Dirks, there were more than 50 resident companies performing in American theaters at its outset. By 1880, only eight remained. The change, however, was not an extinction of the performing arts or artists; it was a reorganization that began to increase the role of management. The reorganization included what came to be known as "the tour." In particular, the railroad system—expanded and improved for the transportation of troops—became a premier way to tour shows and transport the actors that would perform them.

"Touring a show," as we know it today, did not exist before this time. Until the advent of railway transportation, only a star, often an English actor (or an actor pretending to be English), would go on the road. These stars would hook up with regional, local actors to produce whatever shows were in the stock company's repertoire. Which shows were performed depended upon the star, the local talent, venue, and sets, but usually they were classics that everyone knew, such as Shakespeare.

According to Dirks, Dion Boucicault, the Irish actor, playwright, and manager who began performing in the United States in 1853 and later established permanent residence, is credited with creating the modern American "tour." Boucicault pioneered what was called the "combination" company. This new performance innovation combined a company of actors, their costumes, and the sets for one specific play, and took the whole shebang on the road to cities around the country. Not only did touring in this manner create greater novelty for the audience; it also enabled the company to tour new plays. Boucicault also wrote his own. He is, in fact, credited with the invention of the melodrama and was a very successful playwright.

Since the company might have a boxcar's worth of sets and costumes, not to mention the actors themselves, the new and improved railway is what made it possible. Touring productions in this manner became very popular, as it gave companies more work and audiences new entertainment. By the 1890s, local stock companies had all but disappeared.

Booking Agents in the Nineteenth Century: Management or Monopoly?

Regional theater owners needed touring productions and star performers to come to their theaters, but in 1880, visiting a big city like New York to book tours was an expensive proposition for a small, regional theater owner or manager. Thus was born the booking agent, the person who could book the tours for regional theaters. Agents quickly discovered that the best way to create a tour was to book theaters sequentially, only a day's travel away from each other. In trying to accomplish this goal, agents created regular routes, which included a number of regional theaters that could be toured in a circuit. They would then book a series of shows to tour the circuit.

Still, the system could be chaotic. Local theater managers had to rely completely on freelance agents; sometimes contracts were not honored. One agent might not represent enough theaters to create a complete tour season for a performance company. Stars of the day were used to going when and where they pleased, motivated by personal relations with theater managers and venues they liked. Since the star carried the show, the show went where the star wanted to go. It created a haphazard and not necessarily economically happy theatrical environment for managers.

According to playwright and author Wayne Turney, the story goes that several powerful New York City theater leaders—men who were owners, producers, and star-makers, as well as booking agents— met by chance at lunch one day and decided to pool their resources in order to create a more orderly, reliable, and profitable touring process. Their resulting Theatrical Syndicate, also called "The Trust," rapidly evolved into a monopoly of the touring business, much to the consternation of actors (stars, in particular) and theater managers. Because each of the partners represented and/or owned many theaters throughout the United States, theaters, touring companies, and even famous theatrical stars who did not book with the Theatrical Syndicate were left out in the cold. A public imbroglio ensued.

The story sounds inexorably modern: The large corporate conglomerate, wishing to maximize profits, begins to dictate artistic taste; meanwhile, artists and small managers struggle in a financially failing rebellion. The Syndicate kept its powerful grip on the theater world until, at the turn of the century, the Schubert brothers broke the Syndicate's hold. The Schuberts were up-and-coming theater owners headed for great success. They acquired and built a network of new theaters and, notably, developed New York City's Broadway scene. Ironically, they broke the Syndicate's hold only to impose their own monopoly in place of the Syndicate.

New technology, as is often the case, gave increasing freedom to the performing arts industry. The introduction of the automobile helped free the business of touring live stage performances from established monopolies, even as the creation of the film industry began to diminish it.

Americans Embrace the Performing Arts: 1900–Present

Contemporary U.S. government support for the arts begins largely during the Great Depression with President Franklin Delano Roosevelt's WPA (Works Project Administration). In fact two of four arts projects under the WPA, the Federal Theatre Project and the Federal Music Project, established widespread performance and touring throughout America, often in rural areas.

First Lady Eleanor Roosevelt's contributions during the depression era are famous, and the evolution of the modern performing arts center counts among them. During the Depression, it was Eleanor Roosevelt's idea to build a National Theater that could employ the legions of unemployed actors in Washington, D.C. President Roosevelt liked the idea, and eventually introduced a bill to Congress. In it, he proposed a building for the Department of Science, Art, and Literature that would also house four theaters.

Unfortunately, the funds were not available and the idea was shelved, but not forgotten. Furthering the same concept two decades later, a bipartisan law for the National Cultural Center was signed by President Dwight Eisenhower in 1958. Fund-raising was a struggle, though, and the project still failed to get off the ground. It was not until after President John F. Kennedy's assassination that new legislation transformed the languishing project into the Kennedy Center. With $23 million provided for construction, the John F. Kennedy Center for the Performing Arts (The Kennedy Center) finally opened in 1971.

The Great Society

The 1960s was a time of sweeping new arts legislation, and President Lyndon Johnson's Great Society echoed many of the ideals of Roosevelt's New Deal. In the push to enact legislation to eliminate poverty and racial injustice, Johnson advanced a social agenda of better education and enrichment of the culture through art. With the National Arts and Cultural Development Act of 1964, the U.S. Congress laid the groundwork for a new chapter in American performing arts and management. The National Arts and Cultural Development Act of 1964 gave rise to the National Council for the Arts, and the National Foundation on the Arts and Humanities Act of 1965 established and funded the National Endowment for the Arts (NEA), a powerful force for the advancement of the arts in America.

The NEA created a steady trickle-down effect. Because the NEA was required to give a percentage of its budget to any state that established an arts agency, states quickly began to do so. The first were New York and Utah. According to the National Assembly of State Arts Agencies (NASSA), nearly every state had some type of arts association within a few years. In 1973, the NEA's legislation was amended and regional arts associations, in addition to state agencies, became eligible for government funding. Encouraged by this new legislation, regional arts organizations—which were often more effective vehicles to bring the arts into rural and underserved areas—began to emerge. Today there are six such regional organizations, serving the needs of both communities and individual artists across the United States.

As the performing arts grew in importance, and social awareness of the arts created larger audiences, performing arts centers began to make their appearance. Led by the heralded Kennedy Center, these performing arts centers were designed to bring together the best and brightest performing arts professionals and to attract substantial audiences to see them. As in the earliest days of theater, the growth of these centers created a need for more managers, fund-raisers, and other personnel.

The Tax-Exempt, Nonprofit Organization: A New Way to Fund the Arts

The development of the contemporary performing arts community is in large measure structured around the nonprofit organization, which is also referred to as a "charitable trust." From earliest colonial times, charitable activities and promotions of the public's general welfare were free from taxation; in particular, churches were never taxed. After the federal income tax was established in 1913, the courts continued the tradition by recognizing that charitable donations, as well as nonprofit charitable organizations, should also be exempt from taxation. As the public interest and acceptance of the performing arts grew, so did the perception of the performing arts as a cultural and public good.

Charitable giving to the arts tended to be centered on the patronage of individual donors to their favorite artists

Everyone Knows

Members of "The Trust"

The magnates who formed the Theatre Syndicate in 1896 included Charles Frohman, who booked attractions for a chain of Western theaters extending to the coast; A. L. Erlanger and Marc Klaw, who, as Klaw and Erlanger, controlled attractions for practically the entire South; Samuel F. Nixon and J. Fred Zimmerman and his son, of Philadelphia, who conducted a group of the leading theaters of that city; and Al Hayman, one of the owners of the Empire Theater.

or organizations. The Carnegie, Rockefeller, and Mellon foundations were among the first to award grants to nonprofit arts organizations at the beginning of the twentieth century.

In the late 1950s, the Ford Foundation began to give a new kind of grant: an arts grant with a mission. Often national in scope and seen as an investment in America, the arts grant was meant to strategically advance the mission of arts organizations and the arts in general, not merely to support an individual artist or art project. Viewing itself as a catalyst for growth and innovation, the Ford Foundation established the new concept of "matching grants" in which the Foundation would donate money only after the organization itself had raised a substantial match elsewhere. The idea was to help nonprofit arts organizations become established and self-supporting by finding new sources of income and donations. The Ford Foundation model and advocacy had a generative effect on government legislation for the arts, and was a model in the creation of the National Endowment for the Arts.

The Contemporary Performing Arts Manager

Some social institutions, like the Ford Foundation, are founded on the vision of one person with the money, power, or leadership to create something new. Others begin with a raw need. When a number of individuals involved in a common cause or a new industry have a compelling need for communication, support, and interconnectedness, a new institution is born.

This grassroots convocation is the story of contemporary performing arts. In the 1950s and 60s, a new surge of baby-boomers became performing artists. New presentation venues flourished; nonprofit performing arts companies and agencies proliferated; and audiences grew. As the performing arts community grew into an industry, and as government support created larger and more complex venues, managers began to handle increasingly complex tasks; over time they recognized the urgent need to become more proficient and to connect with each other.

In 1956, a group of college and university concert managers, most members of the National Association of Concert Managers, got together to discuss the possibility of creating an organization to streamline and organize performances and tours for university venues. In 1957, at a meeting in New York, they founded The Association of College and University Concert Managers (ACUCM). There were 35 members. Fannie ("Fan") Taylor, Director of the University of Wisconsin's Wisconsin Union Theater, a consistent and influential founding member, served as Executive Secretary until 1971.

ACUCM marked the advent of the Association of Performing Arts Presenters (APAP), the industry's largest service and advocacy organization. Today it is over 1,900 members strong in all 50 U.S. states and more than 15 countries. The development of the APAP as an organization paints a picture of the development of American management in the performing arts. As the community of performers, venues (beginning with educational institutions and spreading to grassroots community venues), venue managers, and grant administrators grew larger and larger, administrators and managers began to organize for better efficiency, better quality, and better training. Communication, research, and education were the keys to success. Its evolution is instructive, demonstrating the kind of vital growth that transforms a small idea into a substantive and enduring organization. Today the APAP continues as a major modern force in research and support for contemporary, live presenting organizations in the United States and internationally.

Training the Modern Manager

In the 1960s, several initiatives provided powerful incentive to increase arts education in America and to establish professional education for arts administrators. Among them was the 1965 The Rockefeller Brothers Fund study called "The Performing Arts: Problems and Prospects; Rockefeller Panel Report on the Future of Theater, Dance, Music in America." Another study, underwritten by The Twentieth Century Fund, was published in 1966 as "Performing Arts: The Economic Dilemma, A Study of Problems Common to the Theater, Opera, Music and Dance." Written by William J. Bowen and William G. Baumol, it concluded that no matter how much study, work, and devotion went into an event, the performing arts could never earn enough money to become self-sustaining. This document was instrumental in the rise of government funding of the arts.

According to Brann Wry, a founding member of the Association of Arts Administration Educators (AAAE) and director of the Performing Arts Administration Program at New York University's Steinhardt School since 1976, "In the late '60s, there was a groundswell around performing arts management education. We thought if people were well-educated in this way, it would help the arts." Among the first to establish management programs for the performing arts were the Yale School of Drama, UCLA, New York University, and the University of Wisconsin. Today, AAAE counts among its full national and international members 43 graduate university

INTERVIEW

Interview: Building the Merce Cunningham
Dance Company

David Vaughan
Archivist, Merce Cunningham Dance Company

**You are Archivist of the Merce Cunningham Dance Company
and wrote a book about the company's history. How did you
get started?**
In my career, I was more of an actor than a dancer. I was in musicals,
like *The Fantasticks*. I studied dance with Merce. I first met him in
October of 1950 at the School of American Ballet—I was taking a class
that he was teaching there. He left a few months later, but he had not
started his own company yet. He started his company in 1953. When
Merce started out, he did not have his own studio; he rented a studio.
When he opened his own studio in December of 1959, he offered me
fifteen dollars a week if I would be his secretary. I was the whole staff
at that time!

How did the business of a dance company work in those days?
We were not incorporated. People had booking agents; Merce had one.
Merce also got performance dates by writing to colleges. There was
no union. Dancers were lucky if they got twenty-five dollars a performance. We often depended on private individuals for funding. That
was before the National Endowment for the Arts. Around 1958, 1959,
the company toured in a Volkswagen bus. In the Volkswagen, there'd
be six dancers, two musicians, and the stage manager/designer who
was often Robert Rauchenberg. There was no real company manager.

programs and 16 undergraduate programs. Sixteen more graduate
programs and 17 more undergraduate programs are associate members, working toward full membership. In order to become a full
member, the AAAE requires a program to have a designated director, a published curriculum, and have graduated students for at least
a three-year period.

University graduate programs in performing arts administration vary in their concentrations, although they all prepare students
for a career in the business of managing an arts organization. For

I did not usually go with them on tour because there was not enough room in the bus.

How did the business become more formalized? What changed?

A few things happened. A really important change was the establishment of the NEA [National Endowment for the Arts] and the state arts councils. In 1964, we went on a world tour. John Cage said to me that we had invitations to go to India and Japan, and a few European places, so he paid me a little money to write to anybody anyone could think of to get more international dates. I wrote letters to people all over the world. It was a real barnstorming tour. When we started off, we had some empty weeks.

I was on the tour because I was the one who put it together. I went as company manager. We got a few grants from corporations and Merce's accountant told him that he'd better incorporate. Things had to be more formally arranged. We created the Cunningham Dance Foundation, with a board of directors. We were the first modern dance company to have a board of directors.

In London and Paris, Merce's work was written about much more seriously than it had been in America. Then Merce started to be recognized as an important choreographer. It was a real turning point. The NEA and the New York State Council on the Arts both started residency programs, and we were on those programs.

How did you become Merce Cunningham's Archivist?

Later on, in 1976, Jean Rigg had become chief administrator. She got a pilot grant from the NEA to employ me as archivist. We were the first dance company, I think, to have an archivist on the staff. That is what I have been doing ever since. I have actually been with the Merce Cunningham Dance Company longer than anyone except Merce.

example, at the University of Wisconsin-Madison, the Bolz Center for Arts Administration (established in 1969) offers an MBA in Arts Administration; the multidisciplinary degree is offered through the school of business. George Mason University offers an MA in Arts Management and one of four graduate certificates: Arts Entrepreneurship, Fund-Raising & Development; Public Relations & Marketing; and Special Events & Festivals. The California State University at Long Beach offers an MFA in Theater Management or (jointly with the school of business) an MFA/MBA in Theater Management.

Carnegie Mellon offers two different kinds of degrees: the Master of Arts Management (MAM), which focuses primarily on the nonprofit sector, and the Master of Entertainment Industry Management (MAIM), which focuses on the for-profit entertainment business and conducts its second year of classes in Los Angeles.

A Brief Chronology

534 B.C.E.: Thespis of Icaria, credited with inventing modern drama, wins the first documented theatrical competition in Athens.

500–400 B.C.E.: Great tragic playwrights Aeschylus, Sophocles, and Euripides, and comic writer Aristophanes, are popular in Athens.

240 B.C.E.: Livius Andronicus translates Homer's *Odyssey* into Latin. Theater becomes popular in Rome as playwrights adapt Greek plays to the Roman stage.

100 B.C.E.–300 C.E.: Comedy is much more popular in Rome than tragedy. Violent public spectacles such as gladiator fights capture popular imagination.

400–700: Entertainment and performance are discouraged by Christians during the Middle Ages, although actors, jugglers, rope dancers, and popular pagan festivals remain.

700: Teutonic troubadours are denounced as their tribes convert to Christianity.

925–975: Ironically, drama is reintroduced by the Christian church as part of Easter services.

1000–1200: Liturgical performance becomes more elaborate and popular.

1350: Liturgical performances move outdoors and are performed by laypeople in the vernacular language instead of Latin.

1405: Constantinople falls and fleeing scholars bring classical literature to the West, inspiring the Italian Renaissance.

1416: The term "ballet" ("ballo/baletti") is coined by Italian Renaissance dance master Domenico da Piacenza.

1470: The printing press spreads classical literature in Italy.

1563: Religious turmoil results in religious plays being outlawed by the Council of Trent.

1576: James Burbage builds the first London theater.

1581: The first ballet is Balthasar de Beaujoyeulx's *Ballet Comique de la Reine.*

1597: *Dafne*, the first opera, is performed in Florence.

1599: Shakespeare's Globe Theatre opens in London.

1618: The first theater with a permanent proscenium arch, Teatro Farnese in Parma, creates the illusion of perspective.

1660: Women begin to appear in French and English theater.

1667: Slavery becomes law. African slaves in the colonies begin centuries of African cultural influence on European traditions.

1730: The first Shakespearean play is performed in the colonies (*Romeo and Juliet*).

1735: Henry Holt brings ballet to Charleston, South Carolina.

1776: The Continental Congress passes a resolution against playhouse "entertainments." Most states outlaw theatrical performances.

1790s: Laws banning public performance are repealed.

1816: Philadelphia's Chestnut Street Theatre is the first to use gaslight.

1828: Thomas "Daddy" Rice, playing Jim Crow, debuts the first black-face minstrel song-and-dance act, further popularizing African-American culture.

1830: Ballerinas begin to make technical and artistic strides in male-dominated ballet.

1842: American-born Ureli Corelli Hill founds what will become the New York Philharmonic orchestra.

1859: The first large America opera house is built in New Orleans.

1881: Vaudeville begins in New York at the New 14th Street Theater.

1883: The Metropolitan Opera House opens in New York.

1889: A production of all African-American performers, *The Creole Show*, opens in Boston and moves to New York. The finale, "Cakewalk," starts a dance craze.

1890: Record manufacturers begin to mass-produce their product.

1895: Moving pictures are invented, a technology that will undermine the audience for live performing arts over the next century.

1905: In Berlin, American Isadora Duncan establishes the first school of modern dance.

1913: Harlem becomes an African-American cultural center with the opening of *Darktown Follies*.

1923: The Cotton Club in Harlem opens, in which black performers play to white audiences.

1926: Martha Graham gives her first New York performance.

1935: Roosevelt establishes the WPA, including the Federal Theatre Project and the Federal Music Project, spreading performing arts throughout America.

1950s: The Ford Foundation creates the matching arts grant.

1957: The Association of Performing Arts Presenters is founded.

1958: Alvin Ailey establishes the American Dance Theatre.

1962: Lincoln Center's Philharmonic Hall opens in New York City.

1964: The National Arts and Cultural Development Act is passed, precursor to the National Council for the Arts and the National Endowment for the Arts. Performing arts organizations increasingly become nonprofit.

1970–1990: The performing arts enjoy a significant support and expansion throughout the United States. John F. Kennedy Center for the Performing Arts opens in Washington, D.C. in 1971. Other performing arts centers open around the country. Universities create programs to teach performing arts management.

1990s: The "culture wars" call public funding for the arts into question.

2000–present: The live performing arts continue to demonstrate resilience, ingenuity, and devotion, with large centers behaving more like commercial enterprises and smaller centers flourishing as part of larger institutions.

Chapter 2

State of the Industry

In 2007 the Americans for the Arts organization examined the non-profit arts economy in 156 communities and regions representing all 50 states and the District of Columbia. The study included 6,080 nonprofit arts and culture organizations and 94,478 of their attendees. Their results show that nationwide the nonprofit industry is an economic force to be reckoned with. "The nonprofit arts industry produces $166.2 billion in economic activity every year," the study states, "resulting in $29.6 billion in federal, state, and local tax revenues. In addition, it generates the following: 5.7 million full-time equivalent jobs and $104.2 billion in resident household income." Moreover, between 2002 and 2007, there was a 50 percent increase in overall audience expenditures and overall economic activity. Four regions, Mesa, Arizona; Miami-Dade, Florida; Boise, Idaho; and Newark, New Jersey, showed over 100 percent increases in economic activity since 2002.

The numbers are something to keep in mind when surveying the struggles of the performing arts community during harsh economic downturns. According to Robert L. Lynch, president and CEO of Americans for the Arts, "What the local and comparative data shows is that not only are the arts a formidable business industry, it is a growth industry as well." However, breaking down the big numbers into smaller job categories presents a challenge in the area of performing arts. Although the federal government gathers and reports some relevant employment statistics in its comprehensive Bureau of Labor Statistics Web site (http://www.bls.gov), many of the numbers group performing arts with other categories. In some areas, performing arts statistics are mixed with spectator sports; in others, arts and entertainment statistics are mixed with recreation.

With that in mind, it is still useful to explore some of these numbers. According the Bureau of Labor Statistics, in the year 2006 there were a reported 83,000 promoters of performing arts, sports, and similar events; 47,000 independent artists, writers, and performers; and 17,000 agents and managers for artists, athletes, entertainers, and other public figures. There were some 121,000 salaried employees of performing arts companies reported, probably a mix of resident performers, administrators, technicians, and other staff. Moreover, a 2002 Urban Institute survey by Mark Hager and Thomas Pollak found that there were as many as 7,000 organizations that presented the performing arts throughout the United States. They estimated that live performances were seen by some six million Americans each week, generating revenues of nearly $5 billion annually.

Employment trends (2006 to 2016) for performing arts companies mix red and black ink. The Bureau of Labor Statistics predicts that the areas of teaching/training, labor relations, human resources, customer service, and advertising will offer the most new jobs. The number of jobs in middle management (public relations, business, and other similar fields) and with agencies showed little change, but the number of new jobs in upper management showed a decline. Fortunately, statistics related to salary ranges for performing arts managers do exist, as the following chart shows. When reviewing this comprehensive chart on salary ranges for five major arts management categories, keep in mind that the salary will be impacted by many factors, including the location of the venue in which the arts manager works, the size of the organization, and the level of community support for the performing arts.

Contemporary Trends in Performing Arts Management

Nobody ever went into the performing arts for the money (unless they were seriously misinformed), and it is safe to say that commitment and love of the art runs high through good times and bad. The 1960s through the 1980s were a boom time; but struggles began in the mid-1990s with conservative politicians' questions about the validity of the arts as a social good. Reaganomics, which emphasized reduction of government spending, transformed itself in the '90s

Statistics from *Compensation Survey Report August 2007* (APAP 3).

M = millions. Av. = Mean.

Number of organizations responding varies by job description.

Budget Size of Org.	Principal Administrator	Second in Charge	Development Director	Program /Artistic Director	Box Office Manager
Over $25M	$180,500 to $475,000 Av: $332,500	$125,000 to $261,620 Av: $194,938	$100,000 to $205,700 Av: $145,300	$82,200 to $150,000 Av: $106,478	$51,100 to $102,650 Av: $69,691
$10-25M	$147,318 to $400,000 Av: $233,591	$99,000 to $185,550 Av: $146,111	$55,000 to $171,600 Av: $80,842	$50,000 to $250,000 Av: $95,634	$33,270 to $98,000 Av: 56,122
$5-10M	$98,664 to $230,000 Av: $157,361	$70,000 to $147,000 Av: $100,340	$46,350 to $175,000 Av: $66,169	$27,040 to $148,000 Av: $77,322	$33,000 to $65,000 Av: $46,430
$2.5-5M	$65,000 to $172,000 Av: $111,198	$44,385 to $99,000 Av: $67,092	$40,464 to $110,000 Av: $66,169	$45,000 to $104,000 Av: $64,801	$36,050 to $79,500 Av: $45,959
$1-2.5M	$44,000 to $165,000 Av: $78,371	$42,000 to $68,000 Av: $53,038	$33,000 to $100,000 Av: $57,750	$30,000 to $39,000 Av: $34,250	$20,000 to $52,000 Av: $34,150
$500,000-1M	$39,000 to $95,000 Av: $61,209	$33,000 to $56,600 Av: $41,625	$28,000 to $50,000 Av: $39,333	$26,000 to $58,000 Av: $43,750	$22,000 to $43,500 Av: $30,722
Under $500,000	$15,000 to $65,000 Av: $44,200	$32,000 to $60,000 Av: $42,333	$30,000 (Only 1 org. responding.)	$27,800 to $42,940 Av: $35,370	$22,020 to $36,000 Av: $26,400

as a rationale to cut government support of the arts altogether. The cause of the arts was not helped when controversy erupted around works of art, funded either directly or indirectly by taxpayers' dollars, which some people found morally objectionable. Some famous examples are the widely-publicized first-amendment/taxpayer-rights clashes and court cases over Robert Mapplethorpe and Andres Serrano photos, Annie Sprinkle performances, and Brooklyn Museum's "Sensation" exhibit. The notoriety of these so called "culture wars" heightened public consciousness of government-funded art and may have led to more questions about the social good attributed to the arts (the fundamental basis for nonprofit tax-exempt status). In such a climate, any economic downturn that tightens the purse strings for all publicly funded enterprises will most certainly result in putting the squeeze on the performing arts—which, even in the best of times, is often tagged as superfluous.

Cautious Optimism

Current statistics in the field of the performing arts may paint a picture of struggle, but there is also cautious optimism. While a March 2009 tracking survey created for the Association of Performing Arts Presenters (APAP) showed serious concern for fund-raising efforts and goals, activity and attendance seemed to be stabilizing. This same survey showed headliner, variety entertainment, and Broadway style shows such as popular musicals holding their own; not surprisingly, new programming—a measure of risk-taking in the performing arts industry—showed a decline. Managers were instituting some cost-saving measures, such as canceling or reducing the number of performances, switching programming to more popular performances, and instituting hiring freezes.

Despite many of these contemporary woes, performing arts communities throughout the United States continue to sound a clarion call to grow, to change with the times, and to endure. Leaders in the field are taking an intelligent and reasoned approach to keeping the momentum going while incorporating new technology, meeting new challenges, and surviving economic hardship. Fund-raising has become increasingly central. One-fifth of all companies reporting to the APAP survey said that they were instituting some kind of special fund-raising effort. Over 50 percent of reporting companies said they had failed to meet budgeted fund-raising goals, with corporate philanthropy showing the greatest (54 percent) decline. Most resident companies reported being behind on their budgets. On the brighter side, some companies reported steady ticket sales.

From Supply to Demand

The subject of profitability and sustainability for the performing arts in a difficult economy were spurs for an influential study begun in 1999 and published in 2001, not long after the events of 9/11 and the ensuing economic downturn. Called "The Performing Arts in a New Era," the RAND report by Kevin McCarthy et al. was commissioned in order to help policymakers and arts fund-raisers better understand the needs and the current status of the performing arts community. It concluded that the performing arts were undergoing a "seismic" shift. The commercial recording and broadcast industries were growing more concentrated and global, the few very large nonprofits were creating bigger and more elaborate productions, and most of the live performing arts organizations were becoming smaller and more local. Mid-sized performing arts organizations, the study claimed, were at risk of vanishing altogether.

On the Cutting Edge

Virtual Tips for Musicians

New technologies allow musicians to offer free downloads of their work. The practice helps build audiences, but how can artists earn a living? New strategies are evolving, including using a virtual "tip jar" for contributions, rallying fans to underwrite the cost of a new CD, and offering (for a price) to visit, hang, or jam with a fan.

According to the RAND study, the likely scenario for the future was that very large organizations would minimize risk by "choosing conservative programming and technology-intensive productions," and small performing arts organizations would become "more dynamic and more diverse," but also more reliant on amateur or unpaid work. Small commercial firms would target niche audiences and move into areas abandoned by larger organizations. Nonprofits would increasingly rely on volunteer labor to produce live performances, catering to local and niche audiences. Mid-sized opera companies, symphony orchestras, ballet companies, and theater groups located outside major metropolitan areas must either become bigger and more prestigious or smaller and more local if they were to survive at all. The implication for young creative artists was that of a narrowing field with less opportunity. The implication for management was, on the whole, that the field would shrink. Well-trained professionals would handle major performing arts centers, but the rest of the live performing arts would devolve to the gymnasiums of volunteer and amateur managers.

The authors of the study urged more research and suggested that policy debate should have a new focus: Instead of figuring out how to support production and performance in the arts—the supply strategies— the arts community and its funders should be figuring out how to stimulate more public involvement in the arts—that is, how to support the demand strategies.

The Capacity of Performing Arts Presenting Organizations

While its concept of audience development (creating those demand strategies) is currently a strong marketing trend in the performing arts, some other findings of the RAND study have been debated. In contrast to the study, for example, a notable 2002 Urban Institute survey and a 2002 position paper from the Association of Performing Arts Presenters took a much more optimistic view of small and mid-sized organizations. Citing an "unanticipated strength in the field," APAP claimed that small and medium sized organizations had "surprising resilience and flexibility"—good news for the up-and-coming performing arts manager.

The 2002 survey of over 800 presenting organizations throughout the United States, conducted by the Urban Institute and funded by the Doris Duke Foundation and APAP, was called "The Capacity of Performing Arts Presenting Organizations." The trends identified by the Urban Institute were different from those found by the RAND study because the statistics came from presenting organizations that were both stand-alone and those that were "hosted" within other organizations (for example, a university or a youth center with a presenting program). By contrast, the RAND study relied on numbers gathered from the U.S. Census Bureau's Economic Census, Federal income tax returns, and national arts service organizations and associations. These contained more information on revenues than expenditures, and did not contain numbers of organizations that were hosted by larger institutions.

The Urban Institute study concluded that small budget presenting organizations dominated the field as a whole, with an increase in suburban presenting. Most organizations were optimistic when assessing their financial health, although negative about being able to provide competitive salaries. Small budget organizations had comparatively lower administrative costs. Surprisingly, regardless of size, most organizations had a roughly equal (50 percent) dependence on earned income and contributions, with ticket sales providing about 35 percent to 40 percent of the revenue. Most organizations did not carry excessive or long-term debt. A salient point for managers is the finding that smaller organizations, often embedded in a larger institution such as a university or community center, sustain greater financial health.

Toward Cultural Interdependence

The APAP also conducted a series of forums throughout the United States, meeting with arts presenters as well as artists, managers, producers, and funders. The findings of the forums together with the findings of the Urban Institute survey led the APAP to define an emerging trend: the cultural "interdependence" of organizations that engage the arts. The findings included that the presenting industry was

➤ increasingly global in scope, with presenters of all sizes booking international artists;

➤ increasingly engaged in commissioning and producing new works;

➤ spreading out more evenly than ever in a network across rural, suburban, and urban areas; and,

➤ increasingly engaged in audience development (especially mid-sided organizations).

Audience development, in particular, seems to be the vehicle through which this cultural interdependence occurs. Through forming new partnerships in programming, education, community outreach, and fund-raising, and by working to improve the quality of arts education, the performing arts community is "embracing creative change" to forge a more vital arts community. Managers in the performing arts need to get involved to understand the community. They need to make their performing arts venue a vital part of the community—not just a source of passive entertainment, but an interactive, dynamic, participatory place to engage.

Creating the Modern Audience

Not long after the RAND study had been published, Michael M. Kaiser, CEO of the Kennedy Center, wrote an influential article that appeared in *The Washington Post*. Kaiser, a very experienced and probably the most prominent leader in the world of performing arts management, identified trends that *should* be happening. In his article, Kaiser proposed a five-point program for performing arts managers. If the performing arts were suffering, Kaiser said, this was the way to make the field strong again:

➤ **Be risky and energizing.** "We have been scared into thinking small," wrote Kaiser. A downhill economy and hard times should not indicate a lack of ambition in the presenting world. Kaiser urged organizations to develop and implement "large-scale, important projects" that excite and engage the public.

➤ **Train great managers.** "There is no shortage of great artists in this world," he stated, "but there is a shortage of trained, skilled managers." A comparison of the funds spent on training performers to the funds spent training the people who will bring them to the public shows a glaring disparity. "Only the most sophisticated managers will be able to acquire the support needed to help their organizations thrive." Those who fund the arts should think about helping in this area.

➤ **Encourage diversity in the performing arts.** Kaiser warned against a trend typical of economic hard times in which only the largest performing arts centers thrive. The "healthy" arts ecology needs "large and small organizations, mainstream and edgy, and of all ethnic backgrounds." Larger, healthy organizations should look beyond keeping their own organizations solvent toward supporting smaller, diverse organizations.

➤ **Promote diverse audiences.** Research shows that the audience for live performing arts is becoming increasingly less diverse. With fewer and fewer children from different economic and cultural backgrounds being exposed to live performing arts, with poor or no arts education in public schools, audiences are becoming increasingly white and upper middle class. Kaiser called for not only efforts to educate young people, but also for more coordination among arts organizations in the effort to reach a diverse audience.

→ **Record performances of merit.** Great live performances, warned Kaiser, are going unrecorded because of the cost of producing recordings and videos of live performance, the collapse of the recording industry, and the lack of resources available to public broadcasting. "It is easier to obtain a recording of Enrico Caruso," wrote Kaiser, "than of most great opera singers today." Artists, unions, PBS, and others should work together to ensure we preserve and share our performing artists with the larger community and with future generations.

Trends in Nonprofit Theater

These days, nonprofit theater managers feel both optimistic and worried. In a time of war and economic turmoil, post 9/11, theater seems more isolated than ever before. Audiences have become more fickle and extreme. As one managing theater director Ben Pesner wrote, "Years ago, people liked things or they did not like them. Now they love them or hate them." Peser goes on to state that it is a wartime mentality. Audiences do not want to be challenged. They do not want their values tested. They want to be entertained. Many managers and actors in the theater feel separated from the community at large.

On the other hand, there are artistic opportunities in the current era. It is a time when people want to belong, when they are searching for something meaningful. In Pesner's report, a write-up of a Theatre Communications Group study, one artistic director described audience growth at his theater as "explosive." Overall, however, theater attendance is down, as it is for all of the performing arts. The competition of other leisure time activities has become ever more intense, and exposure to live performance diminishes as the population grows younger. News coverage of theater performances has diminished, as well.

The "hit mentality" also makes creative, nonprofit theater difficult. Audiences want to go to something that already has a reputation. Or they want to attend a performance where they will see someone famous. Hit shows on the whole are becoming more successful, while more obscure work is faring worse. It creates a pressure for theaters to produce hits each time they produce a play. The decline of government support has spurred many in the theater to call for political action. One artistic director in the Pesner report said, "I am struck by how easily things are taken away from us. If we do not think about political advocacy, we are just going to be spinning our wheels." In addition to political action to increase government funding, administrators in the field are thinking about long-term financial stability: creative capital funding to create endowment funds.

Rising overhead costs, especially for facilities, exacerbates the problem. Health insurance is a universal concern. Touring, a traditional way to make money from a new show, has become prohibitively expensive. Touring productions are either lavish or bare bones—sometimes a one-person show with no sets. Younger playwrights complain that to get a play produced, they have to know the right people. One trend is for young talent to leave the nonprofit theater sector and go to Hollywood. Movies and television provide substantial profits, which means a much higher income for managers and actors.

Theaters are looking to reinvent themselves in new forms: using nontraditional spaces and engaging the community in dialogue before and after shows. The encouraging news is that a new, young generation of performers has exploded onto the scene through new technology. Theaters need to be flexible, and managers need to explore the evolving world of performance that merges live performance with online experience.

Trends in For-Profit Theater

For-profit theater changes and adapts according to the financial climate as well as trends in popular culture. In recent years, film, television, and the music industry have played an increasingly influential role in shaping the direction of Broadway, national touring shows, and for-profit live performance shows. Musical theater versions of popular movies and television shows, as well as plays based on popular screen characters (including animated characters), provide a built-in national audience of all ages and an easily recognized product.

Other trends in for-profit theater include revivals of already proven and established plays and musicals, newly produced with an identifiable cast featuring celebrity actors from movies, television, or other areas of popular entertainment in the leading roles. A form of tribute musical has also found its place in theater trends as a vehicle for creating a live performance show around an already established commercially successful body of musical work. In these musical shows, well-known popular songs are used to tell the story of a famous singer, musical group, dancer or choreographer, composer, or celebrity.

Technical advances also play a significant role in for-profit theater trends. Advances and developments in special effects, lighting, sound, and computers, and the evolution of multi-media techniques in set-design have dramatically altered the landscape of live theater. This, in addition to the fact that modern audiences have become accustomed to the spectacular as seen in film and television and popular music concerts, sets the standard. The use of new technology in for-profit theater opens the door to greater creative possibilities, but it also increases the cost of producing and maintaining a show or of putting it on the road.

All of these trends, separately and combined, have helped to create larger production budgets, requiring greater financial backing and seriously increasing the pressure for new shows to succeed and generate a profit quickly. In this way, current for-profit theater trends are mirroring popular culture mediums of film, television, and the music industry.

Trends in Classical Music

Even though it was called a growth industry in 2001—doubling in size from 1982 to 1992—of all the performing arts, opera shows the greatest earnings gap (the gap between earned income and expenses). A 2000 study of opera by Pierce and a 2001 study by Heilbrun show that opera is increasingly relying on "warhorse" programming, that is, presenting the standard operas everybody knows and loves and not taking risks with new or different music. Traditional operas are greater draws for the casual audience (as opposed to the aficionado), the larger portion of performing arts audiences today. It is the kind of trend specifically addressed by Michael M. Kaiser's call for "risky and energizing" arts management.

Performing arts managers might note a good, statistical argument for the continuation of national funding for the arts. The RAND report and "Performing Arts in a New Era" found that funding *sources* directly influence the health and vitality of performing arts, especially opera. When opera companies received federal (NEA) funding, rather than local funding, companies were more likely to innovate and present more contemporary operas. And in Canada, where public support for opera is much greater than in America, there is no such trend toward "warhorse" programming in opera. Clearly, the lack of federal support (a more global and stable financial resource than local funding) creates a beleaguered environment for the arts in which "risky and energizing" programming seems just too risky. The current trend away from national support toward local government funding may result in a continued conservative trend in opera and other performing arts programming.

Fast Facts

The Recovery Act

President Obama signed The American Recovery and Reinvestment Act of 2009 (Recovery Act) into law by on February 17th, 2009. It provides $50 million to be distributed in direct grants to fund arts projects and activities which preserve jobs in the nonprofit arts sector threatened by declines in philanthropic and other support during the current economic downturn.

Struggling Symphony Orchestras

Symphony orchestras are faring much better than opera companies when it comes to earned income, according to Heilbrun's study. Unfortunately, the better ratio of expenses to income may have something to do with the number of symphony orchestras that simply went belly-up in the 1980s. That is, many orchestras that struggled to meet their expenses finally had to shut their doors in the 80s, creating a trend of greater financial health for symphony orchestras—but at the cost of less diversity.

Although Heilbrun noted that "symphony orchestras have sometimes been described as 'museums of nineteenth century music,'" many managers in today's music field would beg to differ. In a 2006 online interview, Matthew VanBesien, CEO of the Houston Symphony Orchestra, said that symphonies need to find ways to connect to new audiences—people who are doubtful they would even enjoy listening to an orchestra. One way, said VanBesien, is to offer free concerts; another is to offer new and different kinds of programming. VanBesien referenced an upcoming concert with popular singer Wynonna Judd that would be added into the mix of traditional concert performances. Such contemporary programming not only helps to sell more tickets, it opens the door to people who have never seen the symphony orchestra as relevant before.

Getting people in the door is more and more imperative for symphony managers. The Andrew Mellon Foundation Elephant Task Force (EFT) study of symphony orchestras that spanned 2003 to 2008 showed that the "earnings gap" for orchestras was trending larger over the years—not because of economic swings, but because performance expenses were growing three times faster than performance revenues. Managers and leaders in this area were urged to help "orchestras to create for themselves both a vision of a sustainable artistic endeavor and the innovations necessary to achieve that vision." The study called for improvement in four key areas:

1. Community relationships: The orchestra organization should connect with its community and be valued by the public.
2. Internal culture: Relationships within the organization should also become more mutually supportive and cooperative.
3. Artistic activities: The organization should be using its artistic resources to serve the community and individuals in the organization.
4. Financial structure: The organization should set realistic goals and develop new strategies to ensure long-term financial stability.

Trends in For-Profit Music

Prior to the advent of record companies, for-profit music was dependent on dance halls, music clubs, cabarets, and other venues for its audience. With the arrival of rock and roll and the development of popular music culture, live performance in for-profit music became inextricably linked to the recording industry. Bands and leading acts would perform concerts to support the sale of their records and promote their music. As the music industry grew, mainstream artists began reaching larger audiences through radio as well as record sales, and later though music video. Live concerts grew to become so big and so dependent on the recording industry that only artists

INTERVIEW

Filling the Leadership Gap

Sandra Gibson
President and CEO of the Association of Performing Arts Presenters

At the Association of Performing Arts Presenters, you help all kinds of organizations and people who work in the Performing Arts. What trends do you see in the industry today?
One big topic of discussion right now is leadership. Many people are worried about a "leadership gap." When you look at executive leadership in the United States and Canada, the average age of senior executives is about 52. We have an aging senior leadership—who is going to fill the gap? We have been doing a poor job passing along information, capturing knowledge and best practices. There is some anecdotal information, but no system for passing along the practical lessons leaders in the field have learned.

Last spring, a Myer Foundation and Compass Point study focused on nonprofit leadership. When young people were queried about their plans, many of them said that working for nonprofits was not worth it. The work was too hard; there was too little money. We need to retain those people in the industry.

At the same time, many leaders at the top levels of management are not moving on. They cannot leave their jobs! Maybe they have no retirement set up; and then, nobody else knows how to do their jobs. They have not documented everything they have learned about running the organization. That is something that needs to change.

Do you think it is changing?
We are trying to make a difference. We are working on profiles and case studies, developing [studies titled] "Lessons Learned" as well as "New and Proven Practices." All of our grant-making right now is focused on research and development. We are investing in the development of new practices. For example, you take a network of ensemble theaters and try to foster partnerships between them and presenters and regional theaters as a way to develop more mechanisms for tours.

What about trends in technology? Are there new innovations that make a difference in the Performing Arts?
Many nonprofits are struggling to understand the full breadth of technology, to understand how to take advantage of it. I mean not only

Internet marketing and Web sites, but also how to use the technology in the performing arts, what these technologies can offer that is unique. For example, what do online virtual performances and social networking mean to us in the live performance realm? What does it mean about developing audiences? A lot of artists are there, but organizations have not gotten there yet. Many do not have the capacity and the wherewithal to support it; it is hard to get dollars for that. And there are specific audience development tools, advanced database platforms where you can really talk to people, to potential donors. But it is expensive to put these systems in place.

We ourselves at APAP are rebuilding our Web site. We want to get into social networking, to school ourselves and cover more things we do not know about. We are getting more demand for it from our members!

Is there anything going on in the legislative front right now that is significant for arts administration?
Yes, there are a lot of things. I am sure arts management programs cover many of them. But right now there are some things emerging in conversation, and one is: Who should have the nonprofit status? It is heating up into a controversy. The issue has grown out of nonprofit accountability, especially after Enron and WorldCom. There should be a separation of duties and accountability. When there are large endowments, are there payouts that are unrelated to business interests? Or what about, for example, running a shop in a museum that sells high-end jewelry having little to do with art?

Another issue is helping international performing artists. For example, there are onerous laws for tax withholding for foreign artists. And there can be trouble with visas, great difficulties for foreign artists to get visas in time to make their performance engagements in America. In fact, there is a coalition fighting for visa reform, a bill called the Arts Act [H.R.1312, the Arts Require Timely Service (ARTS) Act], which already passed in the House.

What kind of career opportunity is there for people starting out in performing arts these days? You said senior management is aging. Is there opportunity for advancement for younger people coming up?
There is a lot of opportunity, but these days, there can be some stress in mid-career. Sometimes headhunters bring in top-notch people from elsewhere, shutting out others who might have moved up. And, as I said, people in the top roles are staying longer. Right now, it is not as

(continues on next page)

INTERVIEW

Filling the Leadership Gap (continued)

easy to stay in one place and have opportunity for growth. It helps to move around from organization to organization to advance your career.

The important thing to remember is that you have to work your way up. An MBA is not enough. You need practical experience, and sometimes you need to carve out your own opportunities.

Do you have advice for job hunting and interviewing?
What I advise is to do an internship. Do not turn internships down when you get out there. And do "informational" interviews. You call an organization and you say, "I am doing a series of informational interviews; I would like to know more about your organization." Or call the executive director to learn more about the organization.

Any interview or job you do can help, because you never know where it might lead. For example, I had a colleague at the University of Texas who interviewed someone she though was great, but she

signed to a record label could embark on a live-performance tour or create a live-audience event. Today, live, for-profit performances are overseen by entertainment mega-companies and promoters/producers.

As a result, music artists have had to find their own way. In the past, musicians and groups were "developed" by a record company. The company would support the artist in her or his creative enterprise and then produce and market the artist's work. Little by little, the artist was expected to become successful and profitable. Today, artist development is more or less left up to the artist. The for-profit music industry looks for musicians who already have an established audience and a guaranteed market base, ready to go on to even bigger audiences or to an international level.

Over the last 20 years, technological advances and the Internet, coupled with the increasingly inaccessible for-profit recording could not offer him a job right then. She sent out his résumé to others in a broadcast e-mail, and I ended up hiring this guy. Be creative. Go after what you want. Talk to the organization, interview them. And do not give up.

Once you are on the job, what can you do to establish a good reputation and enhance your opportunities?
When you get a job, position yourself for growth. Sink your teeth into the job; when it is done, find new projects to help with. Young people tend to leave; it is like a revolving door. If you are stagnating, find something else to do. This is how I moved up. I was always taking on more, reaching for other opportunities that might expand my experience. Take the opportunities that are presented, just to gain experience, to gain trust. It is just a matter of saying, "I'll do that, sure." Then you have to do your job 100 percent. Go above and beyond. Do not think you are going to hop around within a year. Be realistic. But look for opportunities, too.

Opportunity can come from anywhere. It may not come from your supervisor. Seek out people who are doing things you are interested in. Do not stay stuck in your own department. Get to know the business and how the organization works as a whole. Do you have an opportunity to go to a board meeting? Try that. Do some informal interviews. For me, it comes down to three simple words: Speak, listen, and learn.

industry, have created a critical shift in for-profit music trends. While major popular artists still perform concert tours in conjunction with their record labels and the sale of new CDs, a subculture of independent artists has become a significant force in for-profit music. Performing artists are now able to record their own CDs in home studios at little or no cost. They can market, promote, and sell their music over the Internet, diminishing the need for a record company.

A small, live-performance phenomenon called "House Concerts" has also created a way for independent artists to perform small tours and intimate concert series on their own, where they perform music and also sell CDs. At a house concert, an artist or band will play to a small audience in someone's private home or venue. Advertising is also minimal. Usually, concerts are announced to an Internet e-mail list of fans and posted to Web sites accessed only

Problem Solving

Community Outreach

You work in marketing and audience-development for a theater in a mid-sized city with a substantial Hispanic population. Few if any from the Hispanic community attend the theater, something the director wants to change. You are charged with the job of attracting a greater Hispanic audience to the upcoming production of *West Side Story*, in which all of the female lead character Maria's songs will be sung in Spanish. But you do not have any extra marketing budget. How do you begin?

Your campaign to attract a community must begin in the community. You offer the middle and high schools with the largest concentration of Hispanic students free assemblies and persuade the actor who plays Maria to sing and talk to the students about working in the theater. At the same events, you distribute flyers entitling students and parents to a 10 percent discount on tickets. Some of your limited advertising budget goes into an ad in the local Hispanic newspaper and a radio ad in both English and Spanish. You persuade the managing editor of the same newspaper that a story on the upcoming production and its still-vital issues is worth writing, and you arrange an interview with the play's director. By the time opening night rolls around, you have sponsored more events at local Hispanic community centers—and when your boss sees the audience mix, she congratulates you an a job well-done.

by those in the know. The audience might pay a premium price to enjoy these intimate performances, often meeting and talking with the performers after the show. In other venues, the payment is a suggested donation. While some contemporary artists are happy to make their living in this smaller, independent music scene, others use it as a stepping-stone to access the larger recording industry.

Trends in Dance

More than any of the performing arts, dance represents the melting pot of diversity in today's world. Whereas not long ago, the recognized art forms were categorized as ballet, modern, jazz, and "other," boundaries have blurred in the dance world. Although there is tremendous frustration with the lack of funding sources, there is also great love of the art, new talent, and many who wish to participate in it—a sense of a new "renaissance" in the art.

In 2006, supported by the Doris Duke Charitable Foundation, Dance/USA conducted a series of forums across the United States to discuss the challenges and trends in dance today. Romalyn Tilghman's 2007 "Eavesdropping on Dance Dialogues" sums up the research: First and foremost, different dance forms have different audiences. For example, ballet has an older audience and ethnic dance often has a local, community audience. Efforts at audience development by increasing communication and education, as other performing arts are doing, is also a trend in dance. Another conclusion from the study was that collaboration with non-dance organizations is on the rise. Collaborations might include introducing other arts into dance as well as using dance for other purposes, such as raising awareness for social issues. Dance might be introduced in new places, sharing space in nontraditional venues such as museums, public parks, trolley/subway stops, bars, or community centers.

While dance is often included in for-profit, live performance, dance as an art form in itself is not entirely self-supporting. The difficult market has spurred all kinds of new and innovative marketing trends, especially as Internet marketing has grown, and as dance news, criticism, and education have diminished. As traditional organizations flounder financially, there is a call for increased leadership in the dance community and for greater financial support from the philanthropic community.

A Shift in Funding

Given the difficulty—if not impossibility—for many kinds of performing arts organizations to be self-supporting through earned income, trends in funding are a powerful influence on trends in the arts. Suzanne Sato, in a study of leadership in the performing arts, identified three main priorities for arts programming 2007 to 2011:

1. Investing in leadership: Rather than renew its current endowment programs, the foundation changed its focus from primarily large and a few mid-sized organizations to also include "investing" in small organizations that showed leadership. Its previous investing strategy

identified mostly larger performing arts organizations as "leaders." The new strategy would be to invest in "significant resources" organizations that showed vision and artistic merit, a 5 to ten year history, priority on artist compensation, and strategic planning. Such a strategy would include small as well as larger organizations.

2. Investing in innovation: Innovation—which often is found in small, unknown performing arts organizations that have not yet established a solid body of work—is an important funding priority for the Doris Duke Charitable Foundation. Innovators are exploring the very thing that has caused a big shift in audiences: technology. They are often multicultural, challenge traditional assumptions, the first to "redefine audience as participant, remove barriers separating amateur from professional." That is, they keep the art form vibrant. The foundation planned to renew many of these funding programs and to continue growing this area.

3. Strengthening the national sector: In keeping with the growing body of research and pervasive concern that the performing arts are suffering nationally, the foundation announced its plan to fund not only performing arts organizations and artists, but also initiatives that strengthen the performing arts throughout the United States. Initiatives that promote long-term goals with national scope include research, developing leadership academies, collecting and analyzing data, disseminating best practices, supporting mentorships, and developing networks.

Support at the State Level

A new trend has emerged among state arts agencies in response to the current needs of the performing arts. More agencies are reconsidering their *raison d'etre*—their goals, and methods to achieve their goals. A 2008 study by Julia Lowell, *State Arts Policy:* Trends and Future Prospects, identifies certain practices that state arts agencies are changing:

➜ **Expanding the mission of state agencies:** Since their inception, the mission of state arts agencies has been to fund and support worthy performing arts organizations and artists. Over time, performing arts organizations have proliferated, making it impossible to support them all. At the same time, audiences have been shrinking, becoming increasingly homogenous (white and wealthy) or indifferent and even unaware of the cultural activities around them. Instead of supporting only the creation of art, agencies are increasingly looking at how to support the appreciation of the performing arts. They wish to inspire a more diverse cross section of state residents to engage in and appreciate the performing arts, boosting earned income for organizations while increasing visibility and public support for themselves.

➡ **Forging closer relationships between state agencies and elected officials:** As seen earlier, there has been a growing dissatisfaction with the status quo in government arts funding. Mutual misunderstanding and conflicting goals have seriously eroded government support for the performing arts funding that is vital to the arts' survival. State arts agencies plan to change and strengthen that relationship. Some strategies are "systematic and coordinated public advocacy, more effective use of their board members' political connections, closer collaboration with other state government agencies, and greater willingness to align their goals and their programs with declared state government priorities." The idea is not only to build political clout, but also to reconnect with the community at large—to demonstrate that the performing arts are relevant, important, and for the people.

➡ **Developing new tools:** While agencies intend to continue seeking grant money, grants alone cannot make the performing arts flourish in the modern environment. Other tools of state arts agencies such as convening, matchmaking, advocating, information gathering, leveraging resources, and creating large partnerships are particularly suited to developing audiences, promoting arts education, and growing the creative economy. Arts agencies are looking toward developing these tools, ensuring that "they use all their resources, nonfinancial as well as financial, as efficiently and effectively as possible."

Strategies for the Future

While currently not explicit goals of state arts agencies, according to Lowell, certain strategies seem likely to emerge in the future. Health insurance is a constant stressor for professionals in the performing arts, and state arts agencies are likely to help in that area. Another area of advocacy for agencies is the nonprofit, tax-exempt status of performing arts organizations. As research has pointed out, audience development and arts participation within the broader, more diverse community will be a priority for state arts agencies. At the same time, it is likely that state arts agencies will be funded at lower levels than ever before, and they will need to streamline the grant-making process as well as reduce support for some organizations. While acting upon the generally recognized mandate to expand arts education, state agencies will also be investing in spurring growth in the creative economy as a whole.

Chapter 3

On the Job

Jobs in the performing arts can be as different as the organizations for which one might work. That is, two jobs with the same title (executive director, for example) at two different organizations might entail two different job descriptions. At a large performing arts center, the executive director might spend more time meeting with the community, establishing corporate connections, finding new board members, and supervising the work of others; at a small regional theater, the executive director might spend more time writing grant proposals, deciding on programming, and calling the plumber.

The Categories of Performing Arts Organizations

When thinking about jobs in the performing arts, you have to consider not just the job title, but also the type of organization in which you will perform that job. Each type of organization has its own unique challenges. Therefore, it is helpful to understand the main categories of performing arts organizations in which you might find yourself working: performance centers and theaters; service organizations and associations; performing artists troupes; and with artists' managers, agents, and promoters.

Performance Centers

A performance center is usually a complex of buildings, or one large building that includes several venues, owned and run by a university or a large cultural institution for the purpose of presenting live performances to the public. Such a center might include one or more theaters, concert halls, cabarets, and a performing arts school. Although an old converted barn or renovated factory in a rural community may be a much smaller venue than an urban performing arts center, the management of small and large performance spaces have much in common. As nonprofits, they require fund-raising. As performance spaces, they require maintenance, management, programming, and advertising.

Performance centers and theaters are usually owned and operated by nonprofit corporations as cultural centers. A nonprofit is governed by a board of directors, which is responsible for financial and operational oversight, often helping to guide the corporation so that it best fulfills its mission. Interestingly, because of their size, large performing arts centers tend to be run much like

Fast Facts

Giving Back

At least some managers in the nonprofit sector make enough money to give back when times are tough.

An article in the Chronicle of Philanthropy cites salaries and voluntary pay cuts for CEOs at major nonprofits (Perry and Williams, 2009):

- Douglas Krindler, CEO, Columbus Foundation, cut 4 percent from his $280,000 salary.
- Michael Pastreich, CEO, Florida Orchestra, cut 10 percent from his $175,000 salary.
- John McCarter Jr., CEO, Field Museum, cut 20 percent from his $450,000 salary.
- Laura Walker, CEO, WNYC, cut 5 percent from her $508,520 salary.

for-profit businesses in terms of management organization, advertising, promotion, financial operations, and perhaps even some artistic decisions. As long as they are nonprofit organizations, however, fund-raising and development remains an important part of the overall picture. In addition to presenting performances, most performance centers rent their theaters, halls, and other facilities to the public. The space might be rented for conventions, readings, parties, seminars, or other private events.

The people who manage theaters, performance centers, and other venues are known as presenters. A presenter is an institution, corporation, group, or person who plans and produces a performance in a specific location. The actual performers themselves are not presenters, but are referred to as the artists.

Some large performing arts centers include New York City's Lincoln Center, Philadelphia's Kimmel Center, Washington DC's Kennedy Center, The Denver Center for the Performing Arts, Wexner Center for the Arts at Ohio State University in Columbus, and the Orange County Performing Arts Center in Costa Mesa, California.

Service Organizations

A service organization is a nonprofit group created in order to promote the performing arts in a local community, and to assist performing artists and performing arts presenters. Such organizations, some local and some national, are often membership-based. As a nonprofit, the organization will have a board of directors. This is comprised of people who are familiar with and dedicated to the arts, but also people with business acumen who are able to help raise funds. The members of this board serve for a few years at a time and are mostly unpaid volunteers. Their specific duties depend on the nonprofit charter, but the executive director of the organization is responsible to the board, while the board oversees the organization's finances and operations.

Many service organizations, such as the National Endowment for the Arts and the State Councils on the Arts, make grants to presenting organizations and to individual artists or troupes. Some service organizations, such as the Association of Performing Arts Presenters or Theatre Communications Group, are private, non-governmental membership and donor-supported agencies that support and nurture their members with publications, information, networking opportunities, conferences, and grant-making.

Performing Artist Troupes

The most informal in its organization, a troupe of musicians, actors, or dancers usually starts out as a group of performers with little money and no staff in search of a venue. The lead performer, often the organizer of the group, acts as manager and artistic director. As the troupe evolves, however, and becomes more established, it may need support staff. Even so, management jobs are often part time, temporary, and seasonal except for the most highly visible and financially successful troupes. For example, when the Merce Cunningham Dance Company acquired its first studio in 1959, Cunningham created the first permanent management position for his company. He hired David Vaughn, at the time Cunningham's student, to be secretary. "I was the whole staff," Vaughn, now Merce Cunningham's archivist, says of those early years. Cathy Hernandez, currently Executive Director of *Artes de la Rosa*, tells a similar story. Trained as a cellist, Hernandez began her career in arts management by "helping out" at the Anita N. Martinez Ballet Folklorico, a Mexican dance company with no staff. Before long, after successfully finishing a grant request, she was made the troupe's executive director.

> # Everyone
> ··►
> # Knows
>
> ### Regions Versus States
>
> The purpose of regional arts organizations (as opposed to state agencies) is to help multi-state regional programs operate effectively and efficiently. Often, for example, a company might tour a number of states; when the effort is coordinated, the costs are much less. And a grant for a multi-state tour can be handled by a regional agency but not by a state agency.

Many performing artist troupes and individual artists, including dance troupes, small music ensembles, popular bands, and theater groups, operate independently of any permanent performance space. Often, these individuals or groups will work with a booking agent or manager, developing career and reputation through touring, teaching, and guest appearances.

As a performance company gains popularity and reputation, a performing arts center may invite the company to be in residence at the center. Generally, a resident company maintains its own headquarters and management staff, although the center may help the company with some aspects of management, such as marketing. When the company is in residence at a center, it performs there on a regular basis, usually according to its contract. Such companies also will tour and perform elsewhere as guest artists.

Artists' Managers, Agents, and Promoters

Agents, managers, and promoters represent individual artists or performance troupes, getting them jobs or venues in which to perform, creating tours, negotiating contracts, and helping to develop the performers' careers. Some promoters will work under contract with a venue and book talent as well as manage and publicize the event. Agencies vary in size and are for-profit organizations. Some agencies are very large and well established; many more are small, with only a handful of employees who represent many artists. Agencies often hire interns, a good way to break into the business.

Performing Arts Jobs

Whatever your dominant skills or employment background, you should have no problem transitioning into a career in performing arts management. The field is so multifaceted that people of all areas and levels of expertise, from accounting and finance to education to information technology, are crucial to its continued growth. What follows are brief capsule descriptions of various jobs throughout the industry.

Accounting/Finance

The jobs available in accounting and finance depend entirely on the size of the organization. In a small theater company, for example, the executive director might handle most of the financial operations, such as budgeting, planning, and payroll, and hire a part-time bookkeeper to help with the company's books plus an outside accountant to help with taxes. Larger organizations will have a more active finance department. For example, New York City's Lincoln Center for the Performing Arts lists 21 separate jobs in its finance department, including various levels of responsibility for payroll, controller, accounting, budget analysis, and accounts payable.

Many of the accounting duties in the performing arts are similar to accounting duties in other kind of companies. Money coming in and going out needs to be carefully tracked and recorded to maintain the integrity of the accounts as well as ensure the company's goals are being implemented. Employees will have an educational background in business and accounting. They should also have an interest in the arts. The more strategic thinking required by the job, the more an understanding and appreciation of the performing arts will be important. For a performing arts organization, the finance person is an important link in creating and implementing the organization's long-term goals.

An ambitious career path in performing arts finance might progress from accountant to senior accountant to manager of accounting to controller or chief financial officer. To pursue this kind of career path, the individual would benefit from being a certified public accountant (CPA). To get into the top levels of financial management, it is wise to pursue a master's in business administration or in performing arts administration.

Accountant

The accountant will keep track of the company's money, creating reports that clearly show all incoming and outgoing funds. The number of accountants required by a company depends upon the size and complexity of their organizational budget. For example, at a small dance company, one accountant may be responsible for tracking the incoming grants, ticket sales, and performance fees as well as outgoing expenditures on salaries, rehearsal space, and production costs. At a larger performance center, a number of accountants might track and report on incoming and outgoing funds for diverse areas, such as for a single performance space, or only for educational programs. An accountant usually reports to the controller or finance director.

Accounting Intern

An accounting intern might help with invoice control procedures and month-end closing analysis. She or he will record invoices in accounts payable log and distribute them to appropriate personnel for approval. The intern will assist in the maintenance of accounts payable files, reconcile daily ticket reports to credit card receivable account and credit card statements, update excel worksheets for cash transfers and ticket sales, and create standard journal entries. The accounting intern reports to the senior accountant.

Accounts Payable Coordinator/Associate

The accounts payable coordinator or associate will process purchase orders and invoices, which includes verifying and reconciling accounts, as well as creating reports and summaries. Sometimes the accounts payable coordinator figures out which bills (for example, telephone bills) go to which department, verifies the accuracy of vendor statements, and helps with a variety of other jobs like ledger processing, cash flow and production projections, or budget analysis. Accounts payable reports to the finance director.

Controller

The controller supervises accounting and financial reporting. In some organizations, the controller will take on a larger role, also helping to establish financial objectives and creating long-range priorities for capital expenditures. The controller reports to the chief financial officer.

Finance Director/General Manager

The finance director or general manager in the accounting department is responsible for the entire accounting process, including supervising staff, preparing budgets and financial forecasts for various departments, and overseeing budgets and payroll. She or he will also be responsible for implementing overall financial goals. The finance director will work with the artistic and/or executive director, the producing director, department heads, and the board of trustees on financial planning, budgets, and personnel policy. She or he will often serve as a liaison to various unions. The finance director ensures that the annual spending of the organization is in keeping with the budgets. She or he is also responsible for the organization's tax obligations and insurance responsibilities. The finance director/general manager reports to the artistic and/or executive director.

Payroll Manager/Coordinator

The payroll manager oversees the on-time preparation of payroll and taxes. She or he is responsible for payroll tax reports and will be the point person for all in-house tax compliance issues. The payroll manager supervises payroll staff, keeps current on employment policies and government regulations with respect to payroll, and will keep senior management apprised of any changes. The payroll manager handles federal and state audits as well as internal audits, maintains payroll records and reports, and may be responsible for, or work with Human Resources on, processing of employee benefits. The payroll manager reports to the controller or finance director.

Vice President, Finance/Chief Financial Officer (CFO)

In addition to the jobs of a finance director, the title of vice president of finance or chief financial officer generally suggests a larger strategic role. She or he might take more responsibility for implementing investments, capital-management strategies, and risk management. The VP of finance might also oversee information technology, and work with the development office and board of directors to strategically plan the organization's fiscal stability. When an organization has a VP of finance or a CFO, it usually does not also have a finance director. Instead, there may be a controller, a business manager, and accountants. The VP of finance/chief financial officer reports to the executive director or chief executive officer.

Fast Facts

Salary Ranges

According to the Urban Institute, top management salaries at performing arts organizations in 2002 ranged from $42,400 at small organizations to $123,100 at large organizations. Rural organizations came in at $44,900 and urban at $77,300. Geographically, the New England region (perhaps because there are more urban presenting areas) came in highest at $65,600.

Artistic Management/Artistic Programming

There are two sides of artistic management that could not be more different. Working as an artist's representative, agenting, promoting, or managing an artist is a serious promotional job in a for-profit enterprise. Agents and managers are essential middle-people who bring performing artists and producers and presenters together. The agent or manager represents a number of performing artists and will help to promote them and find them jobs. In a world of nonprofit organizations, the agent and manager are most decidedly for-profit jobs, usually taking 10 percent of a performer's gross pay.

On the other hand, an artistic manager who develops the programming for a venue or performing arts center often works for a nonprofit organization. This job is charged with more executive and management responsibilities than promotional duties, although developing a program that can be promoted and sell tickets is also an important part of the job. Many considerations are factored into programming, including the underlying artistic mission of the performance space, the likelihood of selling tickets, the funding available, whether or not there is a company in residence, and creating a balance in the annual offerings.

On either side, breaking into the field can be tough. Agents must establish a network of connections in order to be able to promote and book their clients. Programmers must be trusted members of an artistic community within a performing arts center or venue, having established a reputation. The best way to begin is with entry level work, especially an internship.

Agent/Talent Agent/Manager

An agent is an almost indispensable middle-person for a performing artist. A talent agent or manager represents performing artists and works with producers and directors who are developing shows and want to audition and hire performers. The agent spends time going to performances and finding new talent to represent as well as meeting and networking with people who produce shows and hire performers: producers, directors, casting agents, and others. Agents are often contacted with specific requests for performers or types of performers; she or he then arranges auditions for people they represent. The agent may hear about a production and pursue the opportunity to set up auditions for their clients. If a client is offered a job, the agent is responsible for contract negotiations, protecting the client's interests, and ensuring that union rules are followed. Agents and managers often work with their clients to develop the performing career, helping with advice and strategy.

The talent agency and management industry is regulated in most states, and often a license is required. Agents are sometimes self-employed; sometimes they work for agencies, which range from small to very large. They are paid a percentage of the performer's gross pay once they have gotten the performer a job.

Booking Agent

Although some booking agents make an effort to promote and manage the artists they represent, strictly speaking a booking agent is someone who represents an individual performing artist or group in order to book performances for them at various venues. In many states, they are required to have a license to operate. The booking agent will know a territory and the venues available, and sometimes already will have a relationship with the manager of the venue. It is the booking agent's job to sell the performing artists to the venue, convincing the venue manager that the performers will attract an audience and sell tickets. The booking agent also negotiates the contract and working conditions for the performers.

Generally, the agent puts a tour together for the performing artist or group. The agent must create a series of engagements that make sense in terms of artists' travel and stamina, as well as the appropriateness of venues. In many states, booking agents are required to have a license. They work for booking or talent agencies, or are self-employed. They are paid a percentage of the performer's gross pay.

Entertainment Promoter

Entertainment promoters are vital to the existence of various types of for-profit, live-performance shows outside of professional theater companies and Broadway. These entertainment promoters are individuals or companies in the business of investing in, marketing, and promoting concerts, shows, festivals, and varied for-profit performing arts events.

Promoters are hired by an entertainment venue, an artist, or booking service and are paid a fee or a royalty percentage of the profit made by the event. The promoter books and coordinates the artists for the event, manages publicity, advertising, security, ticket sales, and door policies. Promoters often work together, helping each other with events either as equal partners or as subcontractors. Sometimes recording artists and musicians act as *de facto* promoters for their own concerts, either directly or through their manager or booking company.

With the rise of corporate ownership of live entertainment assets several large promotional companies have emerged in the field, such as Live Nation and Bill Graham Presents. These larger companies tend to promote more traditional mainstream music in exclusive contracts with concert halls. Alternative music and events in smaller privately owned venues remain in the hands of independent promoters.

Director of Concert (Orchestral/Dance/Theatrical) Programming

The director of programming works for a performing arts center and collaborates with other directors of programming to create diverse offerings for the center. Often a position that requires much travel and attendance at performances across the country, the director of programming will research and identify artists, agents, and producers to invite to the home center. The director of programming will negotiate and administer contracts, budgets, and pricing. This job also involves supervising rentals and relations with resident companies. The director of programming is expected to create a balance of financial management and artistic success. He or she reports to the artistic director or to the CEO.

Managerial Assistant
An entry-level position, the managerial assistant works directly with a list of artists, helping them with the details of their engagements. She or he might prepare itineraries, apply for work visas, arrange travel and housing, process contracts, organize financial information, and maintain press materials. The managerial assistant may also support the department's executive leader by screening and fielding calls and helping with paper work. The managerial assistant reports to the director of programming.

Program Associate
A program associate who works for a performing arts service organization will assist in a number of areas, including grant making, professional development, public affairs, advocacy, and conferences. Duties will include helping with grant applications and grant administration, fielding telephone inquiries, communicating with the public, helping plan conferences, and supporting the executive staff. A program associate who works for a presenting organization will work on promoting performances and events as well as contract coordination, artist hospitality, and helping with the all of the logistics of presenting. The program associate reports to the director of programming.

Programming Intern
Programming interns help to plan shows, assisting with the development and implementation of budgets, ticket prices, and sales reports. They also may help research program options and participate in the selection and contracting process. The programming intern reports to the director of programming or the program associate.

Development, as its name suggests, is the process of finding and developing donors to support the nonprofit performing arts organization. For someone interested in eventually running a performing arts center as CEO, the development office is a good place to start. Forming strong relations with the philanthropic community and being able to raise money for an organization are important and powerful tools for a nonprofit leader.

The development office also is known to promote from within. If a fund-raiser is particularly successful, she or he may have tempting offers from other organizations that would like to augment their own development staff. Further, the beginner in this field can get started by becoming an intern or an administrative assistant in the development office. Another job that lends itself to promotion in the development office is the administrative assistant. If this assistant asks for more complex assignments, he or she will learn the business while making a living.

Administrative Assistant, Development Office

The development administrative assistant performs duties that are much the same as other administrative assistants. She or he manages the director's calendar, schedules appointments, screens calls and correspondence, prepares agendas, responds to routine correspondence, types, maintains databases, arranges travel plans, prepares expense reports, and supports the director in any other way possible.

For someone who has no development experience, this job offers many opportunities to learn about the field and to be eventually promoted to development officer. Sometimes the administrative assistant will be asked to help with basic research, respond to calls, or handle correspondence independently. For someone who is motivated, there are many opportunities in this job to learn about the field of development. The administrative assistant usually reports to the director of development. She or he may also help another director, such as the artistic director.

Development Associate

The development associate may focus entirely on individual and corporate benefit events, coordinating and administering the event and doing the follow-up feedback, acknowledgements, and reports. She or he may also work on establishing and developing long-term partnerships with vendors and in-kind contributors. The associate ensures that the donors receive appropriate information and documentation and will coordinate logistics for a fund-raising event. She or he may organize volunteers; contract and negotiate with vendors;

oversee creative elements; and work with donor hosts to ensure a successful event. In another organization, the development associate may be more of a generalist, with duties similar to the development officer, but with less strategic responsibly. The development associate reports to the director of development.

Development Assistant

The development assistant is usually responsible for thorough and accurate record keeping, including reporting on fund-raising activity, dollar goals, and to-date progress of the annual fund campaign. The development assistant helps with the logistics and details of various fund-raising campaigns, both individual and corporate, which may include help with scheduling, maintaining a database, planning and implementing events, researching donor prospects, helping to write proposals, taking calls, and managing communications. The development assistant may report to the director of development, or, depending on the size of the development department, might be assigned to another officer.

Development Intern

Internship in a development office usually offers a wide variety of experience. It is a great way to learn about the various functions of development and to break into this field. An intern may perform administrative duties such as filing and typing, but will also be given a broader variety of experience and opportunity to learn about development. She or he may conduct prospect research, draft solicitation materials, and communicate with corporate contacts. The intern may be asked to attend a special event or performance in order to greet donors. She or he will usually assist with fund-raising activities including membership fulfillment, corporate sponsorships, planned giving, and prospect research.

Development Officer

A development officer is responsible for specific fund-raising goals, the nature of which will depend on the organization and the type of campaigns that are planned. The development officer may work in corporate relations, individual giving, or on other campaigns, and may be responsible for fund-raising strategy or for developing specific donor prospects. The development officer reports to the director of development.

Director of Corporate Relations

The director of corporate relations works with the director of development to create a strategy of fund-raising from the corporate sector. The director of corporate relations will work to increase corporate support though finding new donors and increasing the level of support from established donors. Fund-raising goals are often established for the year; sometimes they are established by the specific campaign goal. The director of corporate relations may collaborate with marketing and PR to promote and implement a cause-related marketing sponsorship program in support of shows, special events, educational programs, and corporate campaign needs. She or he may also help trustees with strategies for corporate giving. The director of corporate relations reports to the director of development.

Everyone Knows

Educational Backgrounds

According to the Bureau of Labor Statistics, almost all management professionals working in performing arts have a bachelor's degree from a four-year college, and most have advanced graduate degrees. On the other hand, technicians are more likely to have an associate's college degree and vocational and on-the-job training.

Director of Development

The director of development leads the department and staff to maximize the organization's donor income programs. Working with the top executive staff, the director of development helps with strategy and prioritizing the organization's goals; prepares an annual plan for fund-raising; and prepares a budget to be incorporated into the organization's overall operating budget. As manager, the director supervises individual, corporate, public, and foundation gift-giving programs, overseeing the investigation, identification, cultivation, and solicitation of donors. She or he may be charged with strengthening a weak area of the organization's development program, such as corporate giving or individual donor acknowledgements.

If the organization is large and the development department substantial, the director may supervise other directors, including directors of individual giving, planned gifts, corporate giving, and foundation gifts. In smaller offices, the director of development is expected to assume these functions herself with the help of one or more assistants. Either way, the director is responsible for the annual overall fund-raising plan, budgets, and fund-raising events. The director of development usually reports to the organization's managing director or CEO.

Director of Individual Giving

In contrast to the corporate sector, the director of individual giving is charged with managing an annual campaign that primarily targets individual donors. The director of individual giving tries both to increase the level of individual support to the organization, and to increase the number of individual donors. She or he will work with the director of development to set goals and strategies. Strategies may include direct mail, special events, telemarketing, an individual gifts campaign, membership programs, and person-to-person solicitations. The director of individual giving will work with a special events coordinator or other development officers, and may act as liaison with trustees to seek private foundation grants, or to help in other fund-raising activities. The director of individual giving reports to the director of development.

Manager of Development Communications

Sometimes a performing arts center will have a manager of communications in the development office. This person will be an excellent writer and speaker and will support written communications to various stakeholders. The primary function of the job is to develop grant and sponsorship proposals for submission to corporate, government, and foundation organizations. As such, the job is similar to other development directors' jobs, except that the position is more of a generalist and there is a greater stress on supporting the communications of the organization as a whole. The manager of development communications reports to the director of development.

Education

Although some performing arts organizations will have an independent education department—most notably those that have a school associated with the center—the education department is often part of audience development and outreach. As such, it may be a part of the marketing department, or it may be a part of the development office.

Director of Education and Outreach

The director of education and outreach is charged with creating a relationship between the performing arts center or theater and the education community. The education community might include K-12 schools, universities, community centers, local performing arts schools, PTA groups, teachers groups, civic groups, and anyone else in the community engaged in educational activities. The director of education for the performing arts center finds ways to engage the education community and to create educational opportunities for students through performances and special events.

The director might initiate or manage programs that develop teaching guides for performances, coordinate question and answer forums with audiences and artists, or send speakers out into the community. She or he might develop and implement education and training class offerings at the center or create other programs that encourage students to participate in the center's activities, such as a critic's program or a performing arts contest.

As part of audience development, the director of education and outreach may help to develop marketing messages for students and teachers and may implement campaigns directed at the education market. The director of education and outreach usually reports to the managing director.

Program Coordinator for Residencies

If the education department is big enough, there might be a program coordinator for residencies. The performing arts center will hire various artists to teach in the community's educational centers, including public schools, day care centers, senior centers, and other community organizations.

The program coordinator will help to establish residency opportunities and assist with implementing the residencies. Duties might include budgeting, contracting, scheduling, sponsor development, sales, training, and evaluation and assessment. The program coordinator for residences reports to the director of education and outreach.

Executive Management

Executive managers in different organizations display different titles. Some titles indicate subtle shades of authority or executive control. For example, the title of CEO (chief executive officer) usually indicates the single ultimate authority in charge, responsible only to the board of trustees. On the other hand, the title of executive director sometimes indicates a director who shares decision-making with an artistic direc-tor. In other organizations, these distinctions may not exist. A small repertory the-ater or dance company can afford to hire few managers, and there the executive direc-tor may be artistic director and primary fund-raiser, as well.

When seeking to under-stand the corporate structure of a performing arts organiza-tion, it is helpful to view the titles of *all* staff members for nonprofit corporations, usually available on the organization's Web site. Generally, a clear hierarchy will emerge from the list, and titles in different departments will portray a balance of positions.

Best Practice

Take Initiative

When doing multiple jobs for a small arts organization, take the opportunity to soak up all the experience. Learn from every task. If you are asked to do something boring, observe what else is going on and think up questions to ask. "Never be afraid to ask questions," says Cathy Hernandez. "You have to be hungry for knowledge."

The job route to executive management varies. Many ex-ecutive managers and CEOs begin with a small job for a local arts organization. Others begin in the area of fund-raising. Besides a graduate degree in management, one other factor is often common to upper management jobs: the top levels of management rise through the ranks *not* within a single organization, but by taking increasingly responsible jobs at dif-ferent performing arts centers. That usually means moving around the country to where the performing arts centers are located.

In the past, artists often fell into the role of executive manage-ment without specific training. It is still the case that many execu-tive leaders start their careers as performers. These days, however, most go back to school to get a graduate degree in performing arts management.

Artistic Director
Responsible for the overall artistic vision of the organization, the artistic director plans and makes production choices. The artistic director will decide what is performed and who directs it; his or her sensibilities and vision will underlie the artistic integrity of the

entire organization. In a way, the artistic director develops a sense of identity for the performance center, which can help to attract a larger and more devoted audience as well as the ongoing notice of the media.

In some organizations, the artistic director—usually an accomplished artist in his or her own right—may direct productions and may be responsible for hiring a director. For an ensemble company, the artistic director may be responsible for recruiting performers. As with any leader of a nonprofit organization, the artistic director will have a role in fund-raising and developing relations with artists and potential donors. She or he will endeavor to increase the budget and the audience, usually by creating a strategic plan. While the main role of the artistic director is creative, this person is also expected to be a savvy businessperson who can contribute to the success of the institution. Often the artistic director and the executive director share executive powers and run the organization jointly. In that case, both positions will report to the board of trustees.

Associate Managing Director

The associate managing director supervises human resources and day-to-day operations as well as providing support for special projects. She or he might develop and update employee information and orientation materials, create systems to communicate job opportunities, develop staff training, and ensure safety compliance with legal requirements. The associate managing director might also supervise office staff and oversee maintenance. She or he will be expected to attend important events such as opening nights and fund-raising events. The associate managing director reports to the managing director.

Company Manager

The company manager is responsible for day-to-day operations of the staff and company members, supporting and assisting wherever possible. She or he maintains a positive relationship with Actor's Equity (the labor union for theatrical performers and staff) and ensures Equity standards. She or he also administers contracts for staff; maintains the overall theater and production calendars, production records, and files; schedules and manages auditions; manages budgets and payroll; coordinates and assists the public relations efforts; and makes travel, accommodation, and hospitality arrangements for visiting artists and the company. The company manager reports to the managing director.

Executive Director/CEO

In many performing arts organizations, the executive director or CEO is the sole, primary leader. In that case, she or he works closely with the board of trustees on the organization's mission, programming, production schedule, and annual strategic fund-raising plan. The executive director represents the organization to the media and supporters, maintains business contacts in the community, and supervises staff in daily operations.

The executive director has primary responsibility for development and fund-raising, budget management, staffing, marketing/branding, and the organization's strategic positioning. She or he will ensure that the programming and operations remain true to the strategic vision. The executive director negotiates contracts, advocates for the organization and the industry, helps to prepare the annual budget and financial reports, and leads the organization in cultivating donors.

Sometimes the executive director will partner with an artistic director, and they will direct the organization as a team, with the artistic director more responsible for the aesthetic decisions and the executive director more responsible for the financial decisions. Both will work with the board of trustees to develop and implement the organization's strategic plan. In most cases, the executive director reports to the board of trustees.

Festival Director

Many performing arts centers hold annual festivals built on a particular theme, and that festival will have a director. The festival director plans and manages the event. She or he oversees major performances and exhibits; contracts with artists and vendors; designs and manages logistics, show production, and technical production; and oversees on-site management. In addition, the festival director will develop strategies to generate audience development and participation, help solicit sponsors, and support donor and media relations. The director will evaluate the results and produce documentation to assess the Festival. The festival director reports to the executive director.

General Manager

The general manager will work with the executive and artistic directors to negotiate contracts, manage labor relations, and serve as a liaison to the unions. She or he may also act as a key representative for the executive director to the arts community, and assist the executive director as needed, filling in when the executive director is away.

The general manager also works on budgets, participates in internal reviews, helps to manage payroll, and supervises staff. Taking on some human resources functions, she or he will create and maintain an employee handbook and update employee personnel policies. If there are facilities to rent, the general manager will prepare contracts and manage the rental. She or he will also take care of guest artists, booking accommodations and travel and acting as point person. Arranging travel and other accommodations for staff, coordinating social events, and developing production travel budgets are usually general manager responsibilities as well. The general manager reports to the executive and artistic directors.

Managing Director

The managing director works with the artistic director and staff to implement and communicate the organization's long-range goals. She or he may help to develop the board of trustees and help to implement strategies for capital or endowment campaigns. The title indicates a somewhat more hands-on, operational job than executive director with a little more responsibility than the general manager. Instead of being the partner of the artistic director, for example, the job may report to the artistic director. These distinctions are vague, however, and the real job description depends upon the individual organization.

Traditionally, the managing director will supervise the budgets, compensation, and financial operations of the development office, marketing and communications, and business office, and may work with the controller on developing financial reports. In some organizations, the managing director takes on some human resources responsibilities, such as reviewing employee benefits, giving personnel reviews, and developing employee policies. She or he will review all contracts and act as the point person in communications between the artistic director and executive staff. The managing director may report to the artistic director or may report directly to the board of trustees.

Information Technology

The office of information technology (IT) develops, maintains, and troubleshoots technology used to store and manipulate information, mostly computers and telephones. Only large performing arts centers have the budget for a full information technology department, but certain IT functions are vital to the marketing and development efforts of any performance space or nonprofit organization, no matter how small.

In the performing arts, the primary areas where information technology is critical are ticket sales (audience development) and donor relations. In addition to tracking the financials associated with sales, it is also important for performing arts centers to maintain a link with people who purchase tickets and visit the center's Web site in order to develop the center's audience.

For nonprofits, it is critical to capture donor information, not only to track income but also to develop the donor base. Besides database management, the IT personnel will help the marketing and public relations with communications and strategic messaging efforts, such as scheduled e-mails or "e-blasts."

In addition, the finance department of a larger performance center will use IT services for its payroll, audit, and budgeting. While IT work is generally well-paid, and there may be advancement within the department, it is not good preparation for moving into the performing arts. It may, however, be a good springboard for moving on to higher level IT work in the same or another organization.

Database Manager/Administrator

For a performing arts organization, data management might include capturing and managing ticket sales information, membership information, and donor information. At initial setup, the database manager might work with the systems engineer to choose or create a database system that fulfills the organization's needs for data storage and retrieval. Later on, the database manager will be responsible for backing up information and disaster recovery, installation of new software, security administration, and data analysis. The database manager is the person who will help other department managers (such as the director of marketing, or a sales manager) figure out how to access and use the databases in order to enhance marketing and development efforts. She or he will help to use existing data to create new databases. The database manager reports to the director of information technology.

Database/Datacenter Technician

The database technician is an assistant and troubleshooter in the datacenter. She or he works on the daily operations; helps with general maintenance of systems; racks, configures, and installs servers;

troubleshoots servers; runs and tests cables; and performs other scheduled maintenance work. The database technician reports to the database manager.

Director, Information Technology

The director of information technology will take an executive view of this technical department, helping other managers to figure out how to use technology to advance their departments' and the organizations' goals. In addition, this director will recruit and supervise staff to develop, maintain, and troubleshoot systems to keep the organization's infrastructure running smoothly. The director of IT may meet regularly with other department heads, such as the director of marketing and communications, in order to support marketing efforts. The director of information technology reports to the organization's executive director.

Best Practice

The Virtues of Specialization

In the field of the performing arts, it helps if you specialize in one area: theater, international or ethnic performance, modern dance, ballet, or orchestral music are some examples. Getting to know one performance field and all of its ins and outs will make you a better manager and promoter for that performance area.

Systems Engineer

An IT systems engineer in the performing arts is responsible for working with the organizations' managers, understanding their diverse needs, and designing software and/or purchasing hardware that will meet these needs. For example, a systems engineer might help design a telemarketing telephone operation that is integrated with computer technology so that calls can become a part of the marketing database. The systems engineer reports to the director of information technology.

Systems Manager

This administrator is responsible for supervising technical support staff as well as troubleshooting computer hardware and software. She or he may also be responsible for a complex telephone system as well. The systems manager may be asked to do light programming, especially if there is no systems engineer in the organization, and train or supervise the training of staff on the equipment.

The systems manager is a problem solver; she or he is called when the system goes down and is expected to fix it or to know who can fix it. The systems manager is also responsible for establishing and maintaining Internet computer security and data backups, and for installing and configuring new programs. The systems manager reports to the director of information technology.

Marketing and Public Relations

Whether marketing and public relations are parts of the same department or situated in separate departments, their functions are closely allied. The job is to create greater awareness in the public of the performing arts center and its individual offerings, to develop larger audiences, and to sell more tickets and merchandise. Marketing will promote a campaign with advertising and other marketing strategies; public relations will use the media in order to place new stories about the organization and performances. Public relations also works closely with the development department, since the image of the organization and good will of the public will influence corporate and individual donor giving. Like the development office, marketing and public relations are good areas from which to grow into executive management.

Audience Development Manager/Director of Audience Development
The audience development manager is charged with creating a greater public awareness for the organization's performances and increasing ticket sales. She or he will create campaigns and events that often target a new, specific audience segment, for example the young-adult market or the college market. The job might include creating pre- and post-performance events, newsletters, community outreach, and creating and implementing outbound e-mail marketing campaigns. The audience development manager will help to plan and implement each season's overall subscription and single ticket marketing campaigns. The audience development manager reports to the director of marketing and communications.

Box Office Manager
The box office manager implements and maintains the computerized ticketing system, handling subscriptions, single ticket sales, group sales, and box office sales. This manager orders ticket stock, prints tickets, supervises customer service, and may handle customer complaints. The box office manager sets box office policy in conjunction

INTERVIEW

Putting Yourself Out There

Cathy Hernandez
Executive Director of Artes de la Rosa

How long have you been working for Artes de la Rosa?
For about five and a half years. This is the third culturally specific organization I have worked for. I started in Dallas for a Mexican dance company. I also worked for an African-American organization in Philadelphia.

Is this the career you planned on when you were in college?
No, in college I was trained as a cellist! When I got out of school, I was hired to help out at a Mexican dance company called the Anita N. Martinez Ballet Folklorico. After a few weeks, they asked me to work on a grant proposal that was due. We got the grant, and after more successes, they hired me to be their executive director! I worked there for three years.

How was it to be a beginner and an executive director? Did you make any embarrassing mistakes?
No, I did not know enough to be embarrassed. But I was always questioning myself. Now I see I did something right by mistake: I just turned to people and asked for help. I was very honest. People are not intolerant about asking for help; the problem is *not* asking for help but doing things incorrectly. Mistakes can cost time and money.

How did you learn your job?
You just soak up everything. Make yourself a sponge. Ask questions. Use the Internet—it is all there.

You started with a very small job. How do you think people in this profession establish a good reputation and advance?
The best way is to just put yourself out there. You can feel shy inside, but you cannot act shy; if you see a job you would like to try, ask if you can try it. Learn from others in your organization. Ask if you can tag along to a meeting. Go out with the press. Get in on things. You have to be really hungry for knowledge. Let people know you want to try things.

Did you ever study management in school?

Yes, after working in the field for a while, I wanted to know more. I went back to graduate school [Drexel University] and got my [masters] in arts management.

You have a staff of five, including a costume mistress, technical coordinator, teen troupe director, programming director, and development director. What is the role of the board of directors? Do the board members make programming decisions or help with fund-raising?

Yes, they do help. I have a board of 15 people, all volunteers. We meet every two months. The board sets policy; I make sure everything goes as the board wants. I give them a budget and they approve it. Members of the board might change from year to year. If there is an area you are weak in, say legal matters for example, you might put a lawyer on your board. At Artes de la Rosa, we have four main committees on the board: development, marketing, programming, and executive. My programs director meets with the programming committee; my development director meets with the development committee; and I meet with the other committees. We work together like a think-tank, figuring out the best strategies for the year ahead. The executive committee will help nominate board members and scrutinize the budget. My job as director is to make things function, to get the money.

How do you feel about your role as a fund-raiser?

You have to be willing to ask for favors, to put yourself out there. But what is really important is that you cannot be pushy. No means no. And I make sure that people understand it is okay to say no. It is not just about the payroll; it is being caring about other people. If somebody says not now, maybe next year, I put it away until next year. You cannot be overly aggressive. When people understand it is okay to say no, then you do not have to be afraid to ask.

What is one of the most important tools or job skills you have learned to use on the job?

I have to say networking is one of the most important things. Meet everybody, keep in touch with everybody. I still keep in touch with people from jobs I did 15 years ago.

How do you keep in touch?

I e-mail a lot and call occasionally. Also I see people at conferences and work-related events. *(continues on next page)*

INTERVIEW

Putting Yourself Out There (continued)

You seem to have created a niche for yourself directing culturally specific performing arts organizations. How has that worked for you?
Again, that is something I just fell into but it is great in many ways. Having a specialty or a focus can be very useful because you can really get to know your field. After I worked for the Mexican dance company, I was hired as the "Reach" director for the New Jersey Symphony. It was my job to find and attract new, ethnic pockets of the community who did not think about going to the symphony. I find I love this work. You are always learning about new cultures and places. Developing audiences can be challenging, though, especially if people think there will be a language barrier. There are clear differences working for a culturally specific organization. All artists are passionate, but when you add in their culture, too, their passion becomes intense. The audiences are very passionate, too. It fuels me.

with the marketing director and helps to maintain mailing lists. She or he hires and supervises box office staff, customer service representatives, and front-of-house staff. The box office manager reports to the director of marketing and communications.

Communications Manager/PR Manager
The communications manager is responsible for the organization's public relations functions. She or he creates and distributes press releases and promotional materials, conducts photo shoots, and represents the organization to the media and the public. The communications manager is expected to work with other department managers in order to understand the message that should be communicated to the public. She or he may be asked to set up and deliver public speaking engagements or to create special publicity events. The communications manager reports to the director of external affairs or to the director of marketing and communications.

Community Relations Manager

One area of public relations is community relations, and if the organization is big enough, it may have a community relations manager. The community relations manager focuses on developing community partners: organizations, schools, or businesses within the community that will hold or attend events. The events may raise audience awareness for the performing arts center, or they may be events that help to sell tickets. Such events might be receptions, pre- or post-production question and answer sessions, fund-raisers, luncheons, or educational activities.

The community relations manager supervises staff and volunteers, meets with community partners, organizes and attends events, and conducts site visits. She or he reports to the director of marketing and communications and may work in conjunction with the director of development.

Customer Service Representative (CSR)—Telephone Sales

Often a part-time position with light supervision, the CSR is trained to help with telephone sales and handle ticket sales problems and complaints. She or he also might help with general office duties such as data entry, typing, copying, and filing. The customer service representative reports to the ticketing services manager.

Director of External Affairs

A director of external affairs will have a larger scope of responsibilities than a director of marketing and communications, including house management as well as ticket services, publications, marketing, and public relations. In other words, the director of external affairs manages all aspects of the organization's interface with the paying public: the people who buy tickets and attend performances.

In addition to supporting and supervising these departments, the director of external affairs will help set marketing goals, review strategic plans, and assist with hiring and training of staff and managers. She or he will represent the organization to the press and public as the occasion demands. The director of external affairs reports to the executive director.

Director of Marketing and Communications

The director of marketing and communications leads and directs the department to maximize revenue. She or he works with the CEO or artistic and executive directors to develop strategic marketing and public relations campaigns, to raise the profile of the performing arts center, to increase audience awareness, and to increase ticket sales.

The director of marketing and communications will ensure that marketing and public relations efforts represent the vision and spirit of the organization and of the specific performances. The director will work on long-range and annual goals for earned income and develop departmental budgets. She or he will work closely with other managers (such as the director of public relations, audience development, or outreach) to develop campaigns and marketing plans for publicizing the performance center's events and expanding the audience, subscriptions, and ticket sales. The director of marketing and communications usually reports to the executive director or CEO.

Event Coordinator

Managing events is a specific and focused marketing and public relations job. When a performing arts center has active facility rentals for external events, an event coordinator will make sure that everything goes well. Responsibilities include being the point person between the client, the performing arts center, and vendors; supervising the set up as well as the event; and keeping track of event details with appropriate computer and paper work. The event coordinator reports to the director of marketing and communications.

Facility Sales Manager

For a performing arts center, the fee derived from renting the performance spaces is a major source of income. In addition to community organizations and individual performers who may want to rent a space for an event or a performance, resident companies contract with the center on a regular basis each year. The facility sales manager oversees sales and advertising efforts, meets with clients, ensures that event planning goes smoothly, prepares budgets, and negotiates contracts. The facility sales manager reports to the director of marketing and communications.

Group Sales Manager

The group sales manager creates and implements ticket marketing campaigns that specifically target large groups. For example, working in conjunction with the internal education manager, the group sales manager may offer special teaching materials created for a particular production and then target teachers and students. The group sales manager usually develops special offers for groups, develops accompanying sales materials, and finds opportunities for group sales in the community. The group sales manager reports to the ticket services manager or the director of marketing and communications.

House Manager

The house manager takes care of the front of house operations, that is, everything that happens in the audience, seating, and lobby areas. In some organizations, the house manager is part of the operations department, the division in charge of the technical and physical maintenance of the performance space. In some organizations, the house manager may be a part of the marketing and customer service division, perhaps responsible to the box office manager.

The house manager will supervise ushers, porters, and housekeeping, coat check, intermission bars, and security. She or he will supervise staff training, maintain the house management budget, handle payroll, and manage vendors. The house manager may meet with rental clients or residency companies to help coordinate their needs and is the person to authorize the use of house tickets. If there are questions or complaints regarding seating or access, the house manager fields them. She or he acts as liaison with the press as needed, coordinates distribution of programs, manages special lobby promotions, and represents the performance space to the public as needed. Depending on the structure of the specific organization, the house manager may report to the box office manager, the operations manager, or the director of marketing and communications.

Marketing and Promotions Assistant

The marketing and promotions assistant helps with most aspects of marketing and may be in charge of certain promotional efforts. She or he will work on creating and implementing ticket marketing campaigns, help supervise telemarketing subscription sales, and create new plans to increase revenues on the organization's merchandise both on-site and online. She or he will develop promotions with third party vendors to increase ticket sales and build audience awareness, produce a company newsletter, and coordinate volunteers.

The marketing and promotions assistant is a good entry-level position, a place where a hard worker can learn many aspects of marketing and have an opportunity to advance in the organization. This position generally reports to the director of marketing and communications.

Ticket Services Manager/Ticket Sales Director/Patron Services Manager

A ticket services manager supervises all ticket sales, including subscriptions and single ticket sales, and may also be responsible for in-house marketing, such as telemarketing. She or he works with management to set revenue goals and supervises day-to-day sales activities such as inbound telephone sales, Internet sales, and group sales. She or he maintains customer service standards, helps resolve patron complaints, and trains staff in the use of ticketing software. The ticket services manager should be familiar with box office procedures, basic accounting, and computer ticketing systems. She or he will reconcile daily sales accounts and oversee sales staff. Work will often include some evenings and weekends. The ticket services manager reports to the director of marketing and communications.

Web Manager

The Web manager develops and maintains the organization's Web site. Although in some organizations, this job is categorized under information technology, in many organizations the job is seen as less technical and more marketing based. The Web manager will be responsible for content review, Web site updates, calendars, and features, graphics development, HTML, coding, and database creation. The Web manager will work with managers and staff of other departments to assist them in creating a presence on the organization's Web site and adding current updates and information. She or he may also manage a staff and interns. The Web manager reports to the director of marketing and communications.

Production/Technical/Operations

Technical or operations people are the folks who create and maintain the physical space of the theater, including, scenery, machinery, and sound and electrical equipment. They include carpenters; managers; and audio, visual, electronics, and lighting technicians.

Even on the set, people in operations (especially the technical crew) can sometimes work in a world unto themselves. While career advancement may occur within the field of operations (say, from carpenter to operations manager), it is not a field in which one would usually advance into management of the overall organization. Opportunities are more likely to lie in taking on increasing responsibility for technical operations in other, larger organizations.

Professional
Ethics

Dealing with Conflicts of Interest

As a new administrative assistant in the development office at a performing arts center in Lincoln, Nebraska, you are excited about booking travel and accommodations for several guest stars who will be appearing at a benefit, especially since you will be their chauffeur for their stay. A new member of the board of directors, whom you met only days ago, urged you to use a great local travel agency. But once you make the travel arrangements, you find out through a friend that the board member who suggested the travel agency actually *owns* the travel agency. What should you do?

Members of the board are not allowed to profit from their positions. Using the board member's travel agency is a conflict of interest. Obviously, the board member did not know this, or he would have never suggested it. Before you take the problem to your boss, you find some solutions to offer her. First, go online and check whether all of the same flights and accommodations still have openings—which, much to your relief, they do. Next, find a new travel agent you can offer as an alternative. Finally, talk to your boss, who was unaware that the board member owned the travel agency. She is pleased you have already worked out a solution, and she tells you to change agencies. You and your boss agree that she will tactfully let the board member know about conflict of interest as well as suggest to the CEO that new board members get some basic training about the job.

Head of Audio or Head of Lighting

An audio or lighting engineer will head up each of these technical divisions. She or he will maintain and supervise the performance of equipment, ensure that budgets are followed, and hire and supervise staff as necessary. The head of audio or head of lighting will work closely with visiting companies to make sure that their technical needs are met within budget, and that all performances run with proper technical quality. The head of audio or lighting reports to the production manager.

Production Manager/Operations Manager

The production manager supervises and coordinates all technical aspects of production, including sound, lighting, scenery, wardrobe, props, and other special effects, managing all technical or production staff. It is the production manager's job to create the performance envisioned by the director (or choreographer) and producer, insofar as physically possible—and, of course, within budget.

As a staff manager for union employees, the production manager will also be responsible for labor relations, contracts, and workplace safety. The production manager reports to the technical director, the artistic director, or the executive director. In some organizations, there will be a vice president of operations, who will take a larger role in creating budgets, negotiating contracts, and labor relations. In that case, the production manager reports to the VP and has less of an executive and more of a technical role.

Road Crew (Roadie)

The road crew are the technicians or crews that work a tour, usually a music tour. They may be drivers, tour managers, monitor engineers, production assistants, audio/visual engineers, pyrotechnic specialists, or any other specialist that works on technical aspects of tour production. The road crew report to the tour manager. The tour manager reports to the director of the production company.

Running Crew

Jobs included in running crew are those that work behind the scenes during a performance, helping the performance to run smoothly. Depending on the size of the production, the running crew may include an assistant stage manager, a stage manager, dressers, flymen (those who work with the flying scenery used in a show), lighting technicians, a props master, sound technicians, stagehands, and a wardrobe master. The running crew report to the stage manager or the technical director.

Scenic Technician

A scenic technician works as a carpenter for a performance space, using power equipment to produce framing, sets, and finish carpentry. She or he will also load-in (bring the scenery onto the stage), set up, and install scenery, usually breaking down (striking) and loading-out (taking away) scenery as well. The scenic technician reports to the technical producer or stage manager.

Stage Manager

The stage manager runs the show, recording and making sure that the director's instructions are followed and that cues for technical aspects of the show (lighting, sound, props) are maintained. During rehearsals, the stage manager will maintain schedules and work out any glitches, recording the director's decisions, especially about lighting and sound. For a play, the stage manager records the blocking, or records where the cast is supposed to stand during the production, and follows the script to ensure the dialogue is correct.

During performances, the stage manager is responsible for making sure everything in the performance runs according to the way it was rehearsed and intended by the director. With the aid of a backstage communications system, this manager announces the cues for lighting, sound, and set changes, as well as cues for performers. The stage manager reports to the technical director.

Technical Director/Technical Production Manager/Director of Stage Services

Whether a touring production is coming to town or a resident company is scheduled to perform, the technical director is the person who provides all of the technical stage and equipment specifications and makes sure the stage set up goes smoothly and according to the needs of the performers. The technical director is responsible for lighting, sound systems, and any other stage systems used for the performance. She or he will supervise set building and installation onstage as well as backstage and will also maintain dressing rooms. The technical director is responsible for safety and often supervises other staff, including carpenters and electricians. The technical director reports to the vice president of operations or the executive director.

Chapter 4

Tips for Success

If there is one quality that sets you on the road to success, it is this: Always do more than you are expected to do. The successful person does not stop merely because she has finished the job; she keeps looking around to learn how she can do the job better. She is always looking for another way she can help. The successful person never gets bored; he always finds something to learn wherever he is and whatever he is doing. He is always learning; always asking questions; always taking on new responsibilities; always volunteering to try something new; always sitting up front and participating. That means, even more than avoiding mistakes or knowing all the answers, attitude is important. An attitude that says *I want to do more, I want to keep learning* is the attitude of success.

Networking

When it comes to the necessary and dreaded networking, many turn into clamshells. Even the inveterate party hound feels like a mollusk when confronted by the network imperative. For the truly shy, a vision of spending your entire career networking is enough to turn a person to stone. What a deal-breaker! Why not just do a really good job instead? The answer is yes, you have to network! And no, it is not hard at all!

What is Networking?

First to dispel the myths: You do not have to be gregarious to network successfully. A shy person can be the ultimate networker. Because creating a network of relationships is not about being the life of the party. It is about knowing how to connect and keeping in touch.

The discomfort about networking begins to vanish when you understand that networking is not about pitching yourself. Networking is not selling. Networking is not trying to find a job, get a foot in the door, discover the solution to a problem, or promote a product. All that comes later.

Networking is simply about making connections with other people—making new friends, meeting friends of friends, and staying in touch. Networking is striking up a conversation with someone at an airport terminal who is reading a book you like...and then exchanging business cards. Networking is sending an e-mail to that person about a new book you think she would like a week or two later. Networking is all about promoting good will, not getting something.

Why is Networking Important?

Our world is more crowded and clamorous than ever before, filled with people selling and asking. We have become ever more hardened to the pitch, the ad, the schmooze. In such an environment, we need friends with whom to do business. The network opens the door. It is human nature: We trust what we know. We like to help the people we know, and will usually choose to do so over helping a stranger. Helping is mutual, too. We want to help the people who have already helped us. Your network is an opportunity to help others just as much as it is a resource for finding help.

Doing business is easier when you know and trust someone. If you have to choose between giving an important job to a person you have known for a while and giving the same job to a person you have never met before, all other things being equal, who do you think you would choose? Buying a product, asking for advice, getting a referral—in all of these endeavors we prefer to rely upon a friend.

If you are looking for answers and need somebody to help quickly, a network will provide reliable answers 10 times more promptly than cold calling, hiring a professional, or online research. And you may even get 10 different answers to compare and weigh against

Problem
Solving

The Necessity of a Business Plan

Consider the following hypothetical situation: Felicity deLaurent and Ian Kovosky are both incredibly talented dancers that you met in the chorus of a short-lived summer-stock production in Iowa where you worked as an assistant stage manager. You became great friends, and when Felicity and Ian create a new dance company called *Velocity*, they ask you to manage it for them.

Velocity specializes in a unique blend of muscular ballet, acrobatics, and a kind of abstract expressionism created by gorgeous sets, elaborate lighting, and costumes. Ian and Felicity have some start-up capital, and they invite five dancers at predictably low salaries to join the troupe. After three years of steady performing, reviewers from major magazines are beginning to champion the company. You get a call from BAM (Brooklyn Academy of Music) asking *Velocity* to perform. The artistic director at BAM suggests you plan a tour of the northeast, even saying she will help book a few places for the company. Then the unexpected happens: You, Ian, and Felicity determine that the group does not have enough money to fly everyone to New York. Even if you could, some of the group will have to stay with friends or family in the area while a select few can stay at a hotel. The real problem that *Velocity* faces is one that all new business enterprises face: how to grow. *Velocity* started out with a wonderful idea and lots of creative energy, but it does not have a clear direction as an enterprise. The very first thing you must do is to start operating *Velocity* like a real business and create a business plan.

First, Felicity and Ian must decide if the show is a short-term project or if they are in it for the long haul. Once the goal is clear, the business plan must reflect a financial and marketing path toward achieving the goal. The visit to New York and the tour are certainly important stepping-stones toward the final goal, so you must figure out how to fit them into the budget. Find a cheaper way to travel and a way cut down your overhead. Discuss whether it is time to incorporate as a nonprofit. Blundering forward without a business plan is a recipe for disaster. Creating clear goals and using them in order to establish budgets and priorities is fundamental to the art of business and the business of art.

each other. Your network is an invaluable business tool and a great source of personal enrichment. Your network is a chance to give to others, to socialize and have fun, to learn, to try new things, and to do business.

How to Network

Sometimes people confuse *where* to network with *how* to network. Where you network will vary a lot, from a dinner party with friends to a conference with hundreds of strangers. How to network is always pretty much the same. Meet someone you like or at least think is interesting, get his or her card or e-mail address, and keep in touch. Creating connections with strangers is not difficult when you are prepared with a few simple steps. Here is a good five-step method for connecting to new people at any event:

1. **Smile.** It is remarkable how many people are unaware of their body language. Body language announces your feelings and intentions like a bullhorn, clearing the way before you even get to say a word. The crossed arms, the hunched shoulders, the downward gaze and especially the tense unsmiling face, announce that you are unap-proachable. 0. If you are not smiling naturally, odds are you are nervous. Sometimes it is unavoidable. But you *do not* have to share that feeling. Relax your shoulders, take a deep calming breath, and smile. The miracle of the smile is that it helps you to relax in truth. Approach another person with a smile, and they smile back at you. It is that kind of reflex drummed into us since childhood. How rude not to smile in return! And once somebody smiles back at you, it is easier to say something.

2. **Catch someone's eye.** Do not start out by being picky. Anybody will do. You want to meet someone you have never met before, and it is not beauty nor is it panache you are looking for; rather, it is discovery. Try the person standing or sitting next to you. Or go up to somebody who is alone and not talking to anyone. Often, if you let fate carry you, you discover an interesting person who is very different from the person you expected. Another tactic is to ask a friend if he or she knows anyone in the crowd. If you hear about someone you have never met,

suggest finding that person together. The worst thing you can do, of course, is to stick close to people you already know. It is a good place to begin when you enter a new and strange situation, but if you stay there, you will never network.

3. **Say something.** At this critical juncture, the mind has a habit of going blank. That is why it is good to be prepared with a variety of opening remarks. Go for the mundane; a witty remark out of context often sounds contrived. A question relevant to the event or place at hand usually works best.

4. **Listen.** Nerves have a way of stopping up our ears, and it is important to really hear what the other person says. So listen hard. If you get a monosyllable answer to your first question, follow it up with another. The objective is to get the other person to talk about him or herself. Hopefully, a conversation will evolve out of good listening.

5. **Repeat.** Not every encounter will be successful. You may have nothing in common with some people; others may be bad listeners, or totally unwilling to participate in a dialog. That is fine. The object is discovery. After some pleasantries, move on to the next prospect. Sooner or later, you will hit it off with someone—maybe even two or three someones. Those are the people you will add to your network.

6. **Follow up.** There is no point in networking if after meeting someone interesting, you allow him or her to disappear into the past forever. Networking is about maintaining a current list of contacts, so find an easy, reliable, concrete way to keep business cards, names and numbers, and a least a few notes on each person. A Rolodex may be old fashioned, but it is easy and still works well. A couple of notes on the card itself will help to jog your memory so you can picture the person and remember how you met. An e-mail list on your computer can contain personal notes as well as make it easy to keep in touch. (Just make sure you back up this important list in at least two places.) The same e-mail list on your cell phone will make it a snap to text someone when you have a moment of downtime.

Where to Network

Networking is an attitude as much as it is an action. It is about being open to others and making connections. Networking can happen wherever you are. On the other hand, you may specifically want to network at places where you know there will be others in your line of business. That means networking at conferences and association meetings. In fact, there are usually opportunities specifically for the purpose of networking at these events: cocktail hours, luncheons, and dinners. (Using the simple five-step method of connecting at these events, outlined above, makes them much less stressful.)

It also means meeting people at performances and after-show parties. Wherever you work will be an important place to connect with your artists and your community. (Your community should include not only the people who already enjoy coming to your performances, but also the people who could be coming, but are not.)

Expand your network by trying new things in your community that genuinely interest you: new places and new venues, a new cause or a class. A rich source of networking is going back to school by becoming involved with your alumni associations. Get in touch with people you used to know, from grade school through college, and find out what they are up to now.

A great and overlooked source of networking is simply getting to know an acquaintance better. Invite somebody out for lunch or dinner. Take the plunge, even if the water seems a little icy. Almost everyone likes an invitation, even if they cannot accept. You are more likely to get invited places yourself once you have started spreading invitations around. Getting to know your acquaintances better creates a wonderful opportunity not only to deepen a friendship but also to establish new connections with your friend's friends.

Everyone Knows

Get It Right

Making mistakes is human, but there are some areas in which it really pays to check, double-check, and triple-check. And then have somebody else check, too. For example, before you send an e-mail or fund-raising letter to a whole lot of people, get at least one other person to look at your text for possible typos or other editorial problems when you have finished it. "Once something goes out to our members," said Sandra Gibson, APAP, "you can not do it over." Make sure you get it right before it goes out.

What if someone you really want to get to know is seemingly busy all the time? You do not want to seem too eager, and you do not want to become an annoyance. But you do not want to give up, either. Instead of offering the hard-to-get person the same invitation each time, try using variety to tempt with the unusual. For example, you might just "happen" to have an unused ticket to a wonderful show, or you might invite the hard-to-get person to an event where the two of you can meet someone else who is a great contact. Chances are if you are creative and interesting with your offers, that person will finally feel she just can not say no again.

And one last word of advice: Always carry your business cards wherever you go. (Even to the bathroom! You never know whom you might meet in a long line.) Business cards are great to hand out for purely social connections. Because while you write your personal cell phone number or e-mail address on the back of your business card, you are introducing your professional side at the same time. That might come in handy later on.

Working the Net

You establish your network not only for friendship but also for business. You work hard on keeping current with contacts as well as growing the network. So when the time comes that you need something back, work the net. This is the time to ask your network friends if they have any contacts that can help you with whatever it is you need, from finding a great PR person or a great fund-raiser to asking for advice on marketing and search engine optimization. Or maybe it is time for you to find a new and better job. Your network can get you connected. Not only will you get new possible solutions to your problem, you will also be expanding your network with your friends' friends. When your network friend sends the name of a possible helper for you, make sure to add that name to your Rolodex.

Even if you do not contact someone recommended to you, be sure to keep that person's name as part of your network, with a note about who did the recommending and when it happened. Be sure to thank anyone who responds to your request, even if you do not approach the contact. The thank-you e-mail is an important, positive reinforcement, and it is certainly warranted for the favor of sharing a contact. Furthermore, the contact may call your friend to confirm the recommendation; your thank-you note is a good way to give your friend a heads-up before approaching his or her contact.

Social Networking Sites

Some people (especially in the slightly older set) tend to eschew social networking sites because they fear their privacy will be invaded. However, most sites have a series of rules that ensures your personal information does not travel any place you do not want it to go. For example, Facebook allows the general public to see only that you have an account; the general public is not allowed to see your site or view any of your postings. Only after you have confirmed someone as a "friend" can he or she view your posted information. And you do not have to post anything you do not want to post.

Facebook is a leader in online networking. It is an informal social site, despite the newer business pages. Conversation on the site ranges from the mundane ("Hope it does not rain tonight we are having a party") to the silly ("Take this survey to find out what kind of flower you are"), with an opportunity to post and see wonderful pictures of friends' travels and pets. Nevertheless, it can work well for business networking, too. It is a way of personally connecting with many others in the performing arts. You can establish a business page, or create a personal page that you leave wide open for business connections. Business pages are much like personal pages, but instead of inviting "friends," you invite "fans." Anyone can join a business page as a fan. Be aware that if you are networking for business, you should not post information that is truly personal. As a friend's mother used to warn, "Do not say anything you wouldn't want published in the *New York Times*." That includes disparaging remarks about anything or anyone, pictures of your children, home address and phone number, admissions of incompetence, guilt, or confusion, or other negative press.

Some of the fun and silly stuff you can do on Facebook does not belong on a business networking site. For this reason, some people on Facebook maintain two or even three different pages: one business page for fans to join; one personal page used for wide-open, business networking; and one close-friends-and-family-only page. (However, you need to use two different versions of your name in order to create two different personal pages.)

A good way to increase your "friends" on Facebook is to invite friends of friends to join your network. You can also join virtual clubs and make new friends that way. Even better, when you meet someone in the real world and get their card, you can e-mail an invitation to join your Facebook community.

Linked-In is a professional networking site with wide popularity. Very different from Facebook, Linked-In pages, pictures, and information are specifically geared toward business. People are usually dressed in business attire in their photos, "personal information" equals a work résumé, and everybody puts his or her best foot forward. Accounts are free, but upgraded versions are available at a price.

Some people complain about Linked-In because of a special anti-spam feature. If, on five different occasions, you invite someone to link with you and that person responds to your invitation by checking off the option, "I do not know this person," your invitation privileges are suspended. You can no longer invite other Linked-In members to link with you unless you already know their e-mail addresses. In other words, you should only invite people to join your network if you already are acquainted, or if you have an introduction through a mutual friend or colleague.

Some other networking sites worth investigating are:

- **Talkbiznow.com:** Rival to Linked-in, this business networking site enables you to develop your own network as well as explore the user base, keep in touch, and send reminders. It also allows the user to host online Webinars.

- **Twitter.com:** Biggest real-time 140-character blog site going, Twitter is all about what is happening now in short bursts. It has recently become popular with nonprofits as a new way to fund-raise.

- **Quarterlife.com:** A social networking site for people who are engaged in creative work, including writing, drama, music, dance, and art.

- **Upcoming.yahoo.com:** A lively site on which local events can be posted and searched.

Finding a Mentor

Talks and interviews with professionals in the field reveal that along with networking, mentoring is a critical ingredient for success. Everybody needs and has mentors, from CEOs of large performing arts centers to administrative assistants just starting their jobs.

Having more than one mentor is key. For example, CEO Anne Ewers (Kimmel Center) talked about her four different mentors, including one from Wall Street who helps her with financial aspects of the business and one from corporate human resources who helps her with issues involving being a manager of people.

What Is a Mentor?

A mentor is someone who is much more knowledgeable than you and is willing to share his or her knowledge, experience, and advice. A mentor is someone who will stick with you over a period of time—at least until you have learned what he or she has to offer. A mentor is someone you respect and admire. A mentor wants to help.

Sometimes a mentorship relationship develops into a deep and abiding friendship. But a mentor is not necessarily a friend. A mentor is not necessarily even someone you like a lot or would want to be friends with. Rather, a mentor is someone you know you can learn from.

> # Keeping in Touch
>
> **The Central Place of Relationships**
>
> It is all about creating, building, and maintaining relationships, says Adrienne Petrillo of NEFA. That is the key to everything—to fund-raising, to helping others, and to your own career track. E-mail is one of your most important tools.

On the other hand, a mentor must have your best interest at heart, and you must honestly respect your mentor's ability. That is, even if you are not cut out to be bosom buddies, you need to trust your mentor, and your mentor needs to be trustworthy.

Where to Find Mentors

Teachers are often wonderful mentors, guiding students through their first years at work and continuing to provide help, support, and encouragement throughout a career. Teachers are often good at finding others who can help you, even if they themselves do not know the answers. Because they have helped so many go on to professional careers, often they have a large network of professionals who might have experienced and solved a problem just like yours.

Conferences are great places to meet colleagues who might become mentors. You might hear someone speak that you admire. Or you might just meet someone with a similar job with whom you connect. Or that person you meet might know someone else who has a job similar to yours.

Professional associations are also a good source of mentorships. Some associations actually facilitate mentorship. If an association does not, simply joining and participating in local and online activities will help you to meet more experienced people in your field. Once you get to know other members better, you will find people who can give you a hand up.

Do not be afraid to seek out high-profile individuals who would be great mentors. They might be people who have written books or articles you have found helpful; they might be directors of departments at larger organizations, or CEOs of major nonprofits. The important factor is to find people who have what you need.

Finally, do not forget the people you have left behind: your family and friends. Many of these people become more and more knowledgeable the older you get! Family members and friends can help you as well as connect you to others who may be great mentors.

Identifying a Possible Mentor

There are two different kinds of mentors that can help you toward professional success: the "how to" mentor, someone who knows how to do your job and can help you do it well; and the "personal" mentor, someone who has certain personal and professional qualities you would like to develop.

The How-To Mentor

The person who knows your job is invaluable for giving advice— especially in your first year—about how to handle baffling situations, avoid mistakes, maximize your potential, and see the big picture. This is the person you go to when you think you have the right answer, but you do not feel confident. Or perhaps you are confident, but you think you should double-check, just in case.

Then there are also those times when you do not have the faintest idea what to do.

This is the person you can call when you are completely overwhelmed and having a meltdown, the person who can help you sort out priorities and find resources to get the job done. This is the person you will turn to when you have just agreed to do something you do not know how to do, but you have to do it anyway.

Since you need to be vulnerable with this person, it is probably a very bad idea to choose someone in your own organization. Your boss or supervisor, for example, would be an unfortunate choice. The mentorship process is all about filling in gaps, and supervisors do not like to see gaps—especially in people they have just hired. Someone who previously did your job can, of course, offer a great deal of advice, but will there be a price? Is the person completely trustworthy? If this person still works within your organization, will he or she turn around and gossip about how you seem to be incompetent because you ask so many questions? You do not want that kind of paranoia on top of learning a new job. Thus you are better off finding a how-to mentor who is not employed within your own organization. Look for someone in another organization who has (or has had) a similar job, and who has been successful at it.

If your job is so complex that nobody has done anything just like it, try breaking your job down into parts and find a mentor for each part. There may be a financial aspect that a business manager could help you with, a legal aspect that a lawyer could help with, or a fund-raising part that a development director could help with.

Best Practice

Specific Goals

Doug Clayton of LA Stage Alliance advises it is important to be clear about specific goals, since mission statements can be vague. Otherwise, you can get bogged down. "My job is so amorphous. If you have specific goals you can tell if you are succeeding."

The Personal Mentor

When it comes to personal and business qualities you would like to develop—such as how to exhibit calm in a storm, be assertive without acerbity, lead people successfully, maintain confidence, or become more organized—mentors within your own organization can work as well as mentors on the outside. (Of course, if your "how-to" mentor is also your personal mentor, so much the better.) Because these skills are softer skills, there is no danger of seeming incompetent when you are at a loss or do not know what to do. In fact, seeking to grow in these ways might even enhance your reputation as an up-and-coming business person.

Whoever the mentor is, whatever the skills you are trying to learn, one thing must be certain: Your mentor must be good at what she or he does. How will you know? Sometimes your prospective

---

INTERVIEW

Performing Arts Management

Anne Ewers
President And CEO, Kimmel Center for the Performing Arts and
Academy of Music

You have been an executive leader in a number of very different performing arts organizations. What personal qualities does it take to be a successful leader in all of them?
I think first you have to be passionate about the arts. You can do just about anything if you care enough about it. Sadly there are folks in the industry today who bring only the business perspective, who do not have a true interest in or understanding of the arts. As an arts leader, it is important to have a holistic approach, not only an eye to the bottom line.

As a CEO, what have you learned about successful management?
If I were to give tips, I would say it is incredibly important to have a balanced perspective and to present things in a balanced way. I started out by being a Pollyanna, but when people hear only positive things, they begin to be distrustful. Even though you may see the big picture, if you do not share it with others—if people do not see the balance—they can discredit what you say.

I vividly remember when I was running the Utah Opera—at the moment we were merging with the orchestra and it was rocky at first. I had pom-poms in my back pocket; I wanted to keep people in a positive mind-set. I knew the reality. We had to deal with some financial challenges, but we were working toward success. What I learned is if you do not share the down side, people can discredit the positives. They need a reality check. It is better to give people a balanced view than to be solely a cheerleader. Transparency is key. Transparency has been my keynote since the day I walked in to the Kimmel Center. Transparency helps build trust; it moves you forward.

You also need patience. Public perception trails reality by at least a year. You may have turned something around already, and nobody knows. There are so many constituents: the public, the staff, the board. You have to continue to put the message out time and time again until it is understood and embraced.

What skills are key to building a successful career?
You have to be able to listen. You can get so busy trying to get your message across that you fail to listen—to staff, to audiences. When I told one of my mentors that I was going to accept the post, she urged me to spend the first 60 days listening—no major changes, just listen.

Mentors are indispensable. You learn the skills you need from your mentors. I have had four terrific mentors. You must have mentors... different mentors for different parts of your job. I have a Wall Street mentor with a passion for the arts who helps me with certain financial things. Another mentor, my "corporate shaman," is more focused on the use of energy in honing your intuitive skills.

How do you find mentors?
Mentors find you! My Wall Street mentor attended a social event and was impressed when he saw how I worked the room. He decided I had potential and took it upon himself to connect with me and help me. And my corporate shaman mentor was introduced by my human resources director.

Sometimes you get a mentor by stepping forward. When I was a production assistant at San Francisco Opera, even at the first rehearsal I felt the guest stage director was special. I loved how he worked with people, how he interpreted the particular opera upon which we were working. I asked if I could be his assistant director at his home company in Toronto and he said he had no budget for an assistant director. However, he offered me a six-week opportunity with no pay. Supporting myself for those six weeks was the best money I ever spent. He turned out to be my first mentor.

What about planning and advancing your career? Any tips?
You need to be open to whatever happens. If somebody had said to me when I first started that I would be doing this, I would have been amazed. The doors that have opened along the way have led me from singing to designing to directing to producing to presenting. Had each of these doors not opened, I never would be doing what I am doing now. Being aware and available to a door that opens is crucial.

And I think what is most important is everything you do can be a learning opportunity. Never think that anything you do is wasted. For example, as a production assistant at San Francisco Opera I used to be assigned to walk lights—it is exceedingly boring. They need bodies on stage to focus the lights. So I chose to notice the color palettes, and the instrument focus, and the choices made for each cue; I would try to

(continues on next page)

INTERVIEW

Performing Arts Management (continued)

figure out questions to ask the designer. I could have sat there reading a book, or even slept, but I made it my business to come in every day with a question.

How do you think someone establishes a good reputation in this field?
Be totally honest. Be direct. And never give a recommendation for someone in whom you do not fully believe. You can mislead the entity who is hiring and you ruin your reputation that way. When a person asks [if you will recommend them], if you cannot, tell them why. Integrity is key.

You run such a large organization. How do you keep in touch with all the people inside and outside of the Kimmel Center?
I eat Wheaties every day. The stamina thing is unbelievable. I meet with my senior staff once a week and once a week my door is open for anyone in the company to come in. My direct reports meet with me every week or every other week, depending on the needs of their position. I make sure that a board member accompanies me on every single fund-raising appointment. Each board member is also active on at least one committee. I like to circulate in the lobby and greet people before performances, and I go to at least one performance a week as well as every series opening. I usually invite donors to join me in the President's Box for performances, too. I try to combine and consolidate in order to keep in touch with everyone.

If you had to suggest one "best practice," what would it be?
Networking is essential for every aspect of your job. You need to network with donors, people in the industry, and people in the community. Make sure you stay in touch.

mentor is a high profile success. Sometimes you know of his or her success because of being in the field. Sometimes you take time to establish a relationship and you experience another person's skill and wisdom first hand.

Establishing a Relationship with the Mentor

No one busy enough to be successful wants to be approached by a stranger who is going to make some serious demands on his or her time for what seems like no return. So meeting someone for the first time and asking if that person will be your mentor probably is not going to meet with success. However, most people like to help others, and people in the performing arts are very often generous with their expertise. In particular, most people are willing to give a few minutes to help another person who is eager to learn.

The main rule in approaching a mentor is to be eager to learn. Ask for only a few minutes. Start with a specific question. If your prospective mentor is available, ask her or him to go out for coffee so you can talk about his or her experiences on the job, or so you can ask a couple of questions.

If your prospective mentor is very busy, see if you can get an appointment in his or her office and ask for just ten minutes to pick their brain about whatever it is you want to know. (Even the busiest professionals are usually able to devote ten minutes to helping someone else in the field.) If you get your ten minutes, or your coffee, do not stretch it out. That is, do not overstay your welcome. But do ask if you can call or e-mail if you have another question. And you will have another question. And another. In this way, you can develop a relationship of trust while getting to know your prospective mentor. At some point, once the prospective mentor has gotten to know you and you have gotten to trust his or her judgment, you may ask that person to be your mentor.

On the other hand, if a prospect you have just met is generous with his or her time, if the person seems genuinely interested in your situation and in giving advice and you know that this person has a great reputation in the field, you might want to ask right then and there about mentoring.

Whether you approach your prospect quickly or slowly, be sure to always keep the mentor's needs in mind. If your prospect says yes, ask him or her to define the parameters of the relationship. Can you call or e-mail when you are desperate (very useful) or should you meet or call or e-mail at specified times, or (best case scenario) both? When is the mentor unavailable? Should you meet regularly? Your prospective mentor may have strong ideas about mentoring, or the mentor may leave it up to you. If you can arrange it, the best relationship will include a face-to-face meeting on a regular basis to discuss the latest developments (once a month, for example, or once every few months) plus the liberty to call or e-mail when something difficult comes up.

Of course, it is not even necessary to ask someone to be your mentor in order for them to be your mentor. Mentoring is a relationship of actions: You talk about what is going on, and the mentor gives sage advice. If you already have that relationship with someone, there is no need to formalize it with the tag mentor especially if it means that you risk turning what is a warm and friendly relationship into something formal and uncomfortable.

Finally, do not get discouraged if you get a few "No, thanks." Being a mentor is a commitment, and you really do not want somebody who does not have time for you.

Giving Back

Even though the advice is flowing only one way, the mentoring relationship is not a one-way street. Mentors learn from the relationship, too. Even more important, they get the pleasure of helping another person grow in new ways.

What you can do for your mentor is offer enthusiasm and gratitude. You have chosen a mentor; now take his or her advice. Put it to work, see what happens, and tell your mentor the results. Keep the lines of communication open. If you keep coming back with the same problems without having tried your mentor's solutions, you are going to lose your mentor, and rightly so. Even worse, a defensive or skeptical attitude will ruin the relationship altogether. Use the relationship as an exciting springboard to leap off into waters charted by others. It is the only way to learn something new.

Look Before You Leap

One last caution: Be sure you want your prospect to be your mentor before you ask. That is why talking first is important. Get some feedback and see how you like it. Imagine the embarrassment of asking someone to be your mentor, then never calling!

Do not expect to get nothing but strokes, either. Mentoring is about teaching and learning, and sometimes learning means receiving criticism, recognizing mistakes, and doing better. On the other hand, a mentor should never make you feel crushed or stupid. If your mentor leaves you feeling so deflated you can not operate, find another mentor. Meeting with your mentor should leave you feeling uplifted, optimistic, energized, and ready to roll.

How to Advance Your Career

Unless you are lucky, you may have to move around the country in order to advance your career. There may not be many opportunities in your hometown to move up in the world of the performing arts. Once people get into upper management, they tend to stay in their jobs for a long time. If you can keep your options open, including the possibility of moving for a good job opportunity, you will be more successful in advancing your career. Moreover, you may be pleasantly surprised by what you learn by moving to a new area—how moving can enrich you both as a person and a professional.

Get Recognized

Do not be a shrinking violet. Not only should you do 150 percent, but let someone who is in a position to advance your career know what you have done. It might be as simple as just telling your boss. Or it might be something you allude to in conversation with your boss's boss. Or maybe you have got a pal at work who can mention what a great job you did. It is a fine line; everybody dislikes a braggart. The point is that you do deserve credit for a job well done, or for doing more than you needed to do. Advancing your career means being sure that your work is appreciated.

Best Practice

Graduate School or Not?

Increasingly, performing arts managers have graduate degrees in business administration or performing arts administration. Programs that combine concepts of the arts and business are particularly suited to helping young people learn how to lead in the world of the performing arts. Networking and mentoring opportunities abound in graduate school. On the other hand, graduate school is expensive, and nonprofit organizations are not known for high salaries. Other routes to success are majoring in business as an undergraduate, or getting business savvy in the corporate for-profit world before joining the arts community.

Networking and mentoring are both key elements to advancing your career. Your mentor helps you figure out what to do next. Your network helps you find those opportunities. Ask questions. It is one of the most important tools for learning. Every time you see, hear, or read something you do not understand, get someone to explain it to you. The more you know, the more likely it is that you can do complex jobs. That is advancing your career.

If you have not attended business school, read some business texts. This field really requires a consummate blend of skills—one where the art of business is as important as the business of art. Be sure your skills are well balanced.

Finding Your Niche

Initially, your focus within the broad field of the performing arts will be defined by your main artistic interest, whether that is theater, music, or dance. After that, however, your niche is a matter of feeling your way along. Do not be afraid to develop a specialty. There is more opportunity for advancement, and it is easier to network when you cultivate a specific area of expertise.

Often the first job or jobs you get help to define your direction. Most people try to get their ideal jobs when they first begin, but few are successful. If that is the case, do not get discouraged. Taking a job in an unanticipated area is an opportunity to explore your niche. Examine everything you love and everything you hate about your job. Use your experience (and your networking skills) to move on to another job that includes more of what you love and less of what you do not. Often, if we work hard and learn everything we can about our first jobs, we develop an area of expertise. That can help to define your niche.

Your area might be fund-raising, for example, but a real niche would be creating capital campaigns for opera companies or creating direct mail campaigns for new dance companies. Or say your area is producing. Your niche might be producing large, multi-faceted celebrations that include several performing arts around one theme. You do not have to choose your niche; it will develop naturally as long as you adhere to one principle: When opportunity knocks, open the door.

Chapter 5

Talk Like a Pro

The jargon of performing arts administration is as vast and complex as the many arts that administrators bring to the public. The language of dance, opera, theater, music, fund-raising, and business come together here in one glossary to help you glimpse the back rooms, the technical artistry, and the creative underpinnings of performance. The more of the arts language you know, the more you will be prepared for a management job. Use this glossary to look up words you hear on the job, or read it through to get an idea of the language of the performing arts.

absorption coefficient A number between 0 and 1 that represents the ability of a surface to absorb sound.

a capella Music sung without instrumentation or accompaniment, voice only.

accountability The responsibility of the recipient of grants, donations, or public funds to use funds appropriately, to provide documentation, and to keep donors informed.

accounting policy Established by a nonprofit is board of trustees together with an outside auditor, the accounting policy clearly lays out how income of various types will be received and recorded, how expenses will be paid, who will authorize payments, and how financial statements will present assets and liabilities.

accrual basis　A method of accounting in which income and expenditures are recorded when they are incurred, not necessarily when they are actually received or paid.

acknowledgment/acknowledgement form/acknowledgment letter　An expression of appreciation and gratitude to a donor for a gift or service.

acquisition mailing　A mailing to solicit new donors or members.

actuarial value　The value (in current terms) of an amount that will be received in the future as a legacy gift, based on a probable return on investment and on mortality rates.

adagio　A musical term to describe a slow tempo. In dance, a sustained and difficult duet, or sometimes a trio.

adagietto　A diminutive of the term adagio; a slow tempo that is faster than adagio.

ademption　The situation in which a legacy gift is not valid because the assets no longer belong to the donor's estate.

ad-hoc committee　As opposed to a standing committee, an ad-hoc committee is a temporary group created for the purpose of addressing a single situation or problem, after which it is no longer needed.

ad lib　To speak extemporaneously in a show when lines are forgotten or something untoward happens.

advance gift　Often donated by a trustee, director, or organization "angel," an advance gift is a "kickoff" donation to a particular fund-raising campaign, pledged before general solicitation begins. Also known as initial gift, nucleus gift, or strategic gift.

air　A musical term taken from the Italian "aria," a melody for voice or instrument.

alla　A term in music taken from the Italian word that means "in the manner of."

allegretto　A diminutive of the musical term allegro, meaning light and quick moving but not as fast as allegro.

allegro　In music, a term that indicates a tempo that is upbeat or merry. In dance, it refers to brisk and lively movement.

allemande　A German dance in 4/4 time, the first piece in a baroque dance suite.

alto　A musical term for a lower female voice or an unbroken male voice in singing just below falsetto. It also refers to the alto clef written on a musical stave to indicate that the middle line of the stave is middle C. Alto also is a reference to a musical register and of particular instruments that play in that range, like the alto saxophone.

ambient noise   The background sound when there is no sound source.

amphitheater   A circular or oval outdoor theater with raked (rising upward) seating.

andante   A music term taking from the Italian word for walking. It refers to the speed at which a musical piece should be played, a walking pace. Andantino is derived from andante can mean faster or slower, depending on its placement in the composition.

anthem   An anthem is a short vocal composition. A full anthem is for the full choir, with no soloists, while a verse anthem features contrasting solo singers throughout.

arabesque   In music, it refers to short piano compositions of the nineteenth and twentieth centuries. In dance, it refers to a position with one leg stretched straight out to the back while turned out and keeping the upper body straight and lifted.

arco   A musical term for classical musicians playing stringed instruments like violin, cello or viola, indicating that the music should be played with a bow.

aria   A song sung by one person in an opera, functioning much like a monologue in a drama, revealing or highlighting the emotions and thoughts of a primary character.

arpeggio   Notes of a musical chord played one right after another in succession usually from the bottom of the chord up.

arts ecology   The interdependence of the arts and surrounding businesses which support each other with a community.

atonality   Music that does not conform to any key or mode.

attrition rate   The rate at which donors do not renew their pledges or do not fulfill their pledges.

Fast Facts

Rules of Donation

A public charity cannot receive two percent or more of its total support from a single donor within the four most recent fiscal periods. A private charity or private foundation can, but it is subject to more stringent rules.

audience development   The effort by performing arts center management not only to bring in new audience members and to enlarge and diversify audiences, but also to deepen and enrich the performance experience for all audience members.

audit trail   A paper trail that serves to verify financial records.

average gift   The mathematical mean of the funds gifted, that is, the amount of money gifted divided by the number of gifts.

ballad   A folk song or poem of a narrative nature put to music. In contemporary music, a ballad is a slow contemplative song that expresses emotion.

bargain sale   The sale of property to a nonprofit organization at below market value, which makes it partly a sale and partly a gift.

baritone   A male voice that is lower than a tenor but higher than a bass. It also describes a pitched brass instrument of a low register like a baritone saxophone.

baroque   A term in musicology used to designate a period in music 1600–1750.

bass   A musical term that denotes the lowest register. In singing and opera, it is the lowest male voice. It is also used as an adjective to define lower register instruments like the bass clarinet. Bass is also a musical term for "double bass," the lowest of the string instruments. In brass bands, bass is the name used for the orchestral tuba.

bass-baritone   A male voice who sings in both bass and baritone registers.

bassoon   A double reed wind instrument. It also the bass of the woodwind section of an orchestra.

bellwether   A gift or action that sets a standard in a fund-raising campaign.

benefactor   A generous donor, often the highest level of gifting.

bequest   Something given or left in a will.

berceuse   In classical music, a term for a cradle song or lullaby.

bitonality   The juxtaposition of two different keys of music (for example C major and F minor) or modes of music playing at the same time.

bleed   In printing, any copy or illustration that continues to the edge of the page without any margin.

blue note   In music, a note in a blues scale that is dissonant with the other notes, thus producing a tension when it is played.

board of directors or **board of trustees**   The people selected to serve as a governing body of a nonprofit organization. They are responsible for fiscal oversight as well as for helping to guide management. For many nonprofits, the board will help to fund-raise, and might contribute financially to the organization themselves. The organization's CEO is responsible to the board. The board members are volunteers and are not compensated and should not profit in any way from their service on the board.

boilerplate   Text of a fund-raising letter or other document that is generic and can be used as a basis for more personalized messages.

bolero   A Spanish dance popular in France and Latin America. It is also the title of a composition by Ravel.

bona fide pledge   A financial pledge that is in some way shown to be real. It may be documented, publicly announced, or partially paid.

bricks-and-mortar campaign   A fund-raising effort to raise funds for building construction.

bridge   A walkway above a stage used for access to lighting and technical equipment. Also called catwalk.

bridge loan   A loan that will help an organization sustain itself or a program until the actual grant or funding arrives.

brio   A musical term meaning vivacity, fire, brilliance, and energy.

Broadway   Used to denote not only New York City's Broadway, but also popular musical shows performed at any venue.

bulk rate mail   For soliciting members and donations, a large quantity of presorted mail that goes out at a reduced, bulk postage rate.

bump   A flash or sudden brightening of stage lighting.

bundle   To sort mail by zip code.

business plan   A document that identifies a business' long and short-term goals and defines the specific steps that will be taken to achieve them, including financial projections of income and expenses.

bylaws   Rules adopted by a board of trustees by which the board itself are governed.

cadence   A term for a kind of musical punctuation usually made up of two chords played at the end of a musical phrase.

cadenza   A classical music term for an extended and embellished final cadence often leading to the last section of a movement.

caging   The collection of pledges (that is, collecting the actual cash) made to a nonprofit organization by another entity.

camera A musical term from the phrase "sonata da camera" which is a secular sonata for dance and separate from church sonatas.

campaign An organized effort to raise funds for a specific purpose.

canon Counterpoint melody in which melody is introduced by a voice or instrument and then is imitated by one or more other voices or instruments in the manner of a round.

canon focused A repertoire that is centered mostly on old favorites and does not take risks with newer works.

cantata A choral musical work for voice and accompanying instrumentation.

capability statement An evaluation of how well an organization is able to live up to its mission statement and goals.

capacity The ability to perform or produce a desired output or product; a measure of the ability of a center to bring the performing arts to the public.

capacity development To enlarge, in a variety of ways, the capability of a performing arts center to present the performing arts to the public.

capital asset Any asset that is invested and held over the long-term in order to realize a profit.

capriccio A term with different musical meanings depending on the composer and period. In the 16th and 17th centuries it indicated a fugal composition and then later came to signify a dance or dance suite.

carry over With reference to a charitable gift that is above the tax-deductible limit allowed by law in one year, to carry forward the balance and spread the amount over several years.

case statement A presentation that puts for the reasons an organization needs and deserves philanthropic support.

categorical grant A grant that is given only for a specific program in a certain category.

catwalk A walkway above a stage used for access to lighting and technical equipment. Also called a bridge.

cause-related marketing A marketing campaign in which a for-profit company, in return for giving a portion of its sales to a nonprofit organization, can use the nonprofit's name and cause to help sell its product.

celesta A small keyboard using hammers striking metal bars to create a ringing sound, developed in the nineteenth century.

chaconne   A term that originated from the word for a dance in Spain in the seventeenth century. In music, it denotes a series of variations over a short repeated bass or chord pattern.

challenge gift/challenge grant   Meant to spur the public to give more, a challenge grant is a gift to a nonprofit organization that is conditional upon the organization raising a certain amount from the public within a prescribed period of time.

chamber music   Music for a small ensemble of instruments. A composition originally created for performance in a room or "chamber."

chamber orchestra   A term for an orchestra smaller than a symphony orchestra.

changes   A term in jazz and popular music serving as an abbreviation for "chord changes," which serve as the harmonic progression on which melody is based.

chanson   A French song, also a reference to troubadour compositions of the Middle Ages and art songs of the nineteenth century.

chapel   In music, a term that means a group of musicians performing for the church or employed by a musical establishment (for example, the English Chapel Royale).

charitable-gift annuity   A gift of cash or property to a charitable nonprofit which stipulates a certain fixed payment to the donor or other beneficiary at regular predetermined intervals.

charitable lead trust   A trust fund that pays a stream of revenue to a charity for a fixed term, at the end of which the fund is distributed to non-charitable beneficiaries (for example, grandchildren).

charitable remainder trust   A trust fund that pays a specified amount to one or more individuals for a specific term, with the remainder to go to a charity.

charitable trust   A trust fund established to benefit one or more charities.

cheshire labels   Mailing labels that are computer printed, cut with a Cheshire machine, and affixed with glue. They are usually about half the price of pressure labels.

chops   A slang term in music referring to a musician's proficiency on their instrument.

chorale   A hymn or tune adapted to various harmonies of a composition. It also refers to a group of singers in a choir or chorus.

chord   The simultaneous sounding of two or more notes together. How these notes relate to each other and create a separate tone or sound is the study of harmony.

circulating capital   Funds that are in use to purchase or pay, in contrast to fixed capital, or invested funds.

closed corporation   A privately held business in which the stock is held by only one person or a few people, often within one family.

coda   In music, a closing section within a composition.

code   In fund-raising, a symbol or word used to distinguish returns on various mailings.

coloratura   In opera and classical music, a coloration or elaboration of a vocal line or a type of soprano voice.

commercial co-venturer   A for-profit commercial partner who advertises that sale or use of its product will benefit a charitable nonprofit.

common time   Time signature 4/4 which is four beats per measure, each beat a quarter note in length.

communication audit   A review to ascertain whether or not a particular public relations program is having the desired effect.

contact code   In fund-raising, a symbol or word that specifies the way in which someone prefers to be contacted.

control package   The package in a mailing that will be used as a benchmark against which other mailings will be measured.

cookie   A piece of computer code that a Web site you visit places upon your computer. The cookie identifies your computer and information about your preferences so that when you log into that site again, you are presented with personalized information or sales pitches.

corporate foundation   A foundation created for charitable giving, owned and funded by a for-profit corporation.

corporate giving program   A program of charitable giving by a corporation, or a program of soliciting funds from a corporation by a charitable organization.

corporate veil   The concept that members of a nonprofit corporation are not responsible for the corporate debt beyond their original commitments.

corpus   The principal of a trust, as opposed to the income.

cost disease   A theory proposed by Baumol and Bowen in their classic 1966 study of the economics of the performing arts. "Cost disease" stipulates that since the performing arts can not employ technology to replace increasingly expensive performing artists and thereby reduce costs (as other businesses will), the costs of producing performances will rise faster than costs in the general business arena.

creative economy   The total economy surrounding creative enterprises. For example, the creative economy might include the restaurant, tourist, transportation, and shopping trade generated around a performing arts center in addition to the center's ticket sales.

crescendo   A musical term for a sound progressively growing louder.

critical path   The important stages of a project that are used to figure out the project's minimum time frame.

cultivate   To engage and involve potential donors, volunteers, and supporters in the people, programs, and plans of the nonprofit organization.

cultivation event or material   Events or literature created to spur interest in and enthusiasm for a nonprofit or its programs.

cultural identity   The culture with which one identifies through cultural activities and membership.

cultural purchase   Things that are bought as part of a person's cultural choices, such as performing arts tickets, books, and CDs.

customer relationship management (CRM)   Developing relationships with individual customers, getting to know their interests, needs, and preferences, and thus being able to provide more of what they want and less of what they do not want. Also known as relationship marketing.

cut time   A musical term that indicates two half note beats per measure (meter 2/2), notated and played like common time (4/4) except with the beat lengths doubled.

da capo   A musical notation that indicates "from the beginning."

database   Information that is stored on computer in a systematized way so that various programs can retrieve the data for different uses.

decentralized fund-raising   A process by which various parts of an organization fund-raise instead of fund-raising activities proceeding from a centralized office.

de-dupe   To remove duplicate names from a mailing list.

demand strategies   As opposed to supply strategies, business strategies that focus on creating a bigger demand for the product. See also audience development.

demonstration grant A grant awarded with the understanding that the program funded will serve as a model.

designated fund Usually structured as an endowment, this fund is held by a charitable organization that makes distributions to other charitable organizations.

development Refers to the overall process of acquainting the public with the nonprofit organization's mission and raising funds to support the organization's programs.

diminuendo A musical term that means gradually decreasing volume, dwindling.

direct cost In accounting, a cost that can be attributed to a specific program, as opposed to general overhead costs.

direct mail Mass mailings to solicit funds or support.

dissonance In music, a combination of notes that sound harsh or create tension when played together.

D.S. al fine A term in music notation that means "from the sign to the end."

dues level The level of membership defined by services as well as dues paid.

dynamics In music, a term that refers to the relative volumes in a piece of music.

earmark To specify a particular purpose for a specific fund or amount of money.

earned income As opposed to gifted, interest, or other unearned income, money that is earned by sales of goods, products, or services.

earnings gap The gap between a performing arts venue's earned income (from tickets and other sales) and its expenses. For nonprofits, the earnings gap is typically filled by donor gifts or other unearned income.

EIN Employer Identification Number, assigned by the federal government to every corporation for the purpose of reporting employee income.

eco A musical effect in which a group of notes is repeated to create an echo effect.

electronic screening A process by which an organization's database may be compared to a larger database in order to get more information on names, such as addresses, household information, and likelihood of giving.

eleemosynary Pertaining to, or dependent upon, charity.

end on   The traditional layout of a theater in which the audience is seated looking all in one direction at the stage through the proscenium arch.

endowment   A gift of money to a nonprofit that is invested and produces income. The capital is protected and only the income is spent, either according to the wishes of the donor or the board of trustees.

endowment campaign   A fund-raising campaign for the purpose of creating or increasing an organization's endowment.

en face   A term used in dance referring to a position on stage facing directly forward.

executive committee   A subset of the board of trustees that is granted authority to govern the nonprofit between meetings of the full board.

exempt purpose   The action or cause for an organization to be granted charitable, nonprofit tax-exempt status.

external affairs   The relations of an organization with the community, customers, and patrons, or anyone outside the board and staff of the organization itself.

fact sheet   A fact sheet, created to acquaint volunteers with a campaign, should summarize the nonprofit is mission, goals, and programs.

fair market value   The price that something would bring if it were offered for sale on the open market.

fair share   An amount of giving suggested based upon a donor's potential.

falsetto   A term in music for when a male voice is singing above tenor range.

fermata   A rest or note that is at the end of a section, movement or composition whereby the performer or conductor prolongs the ending note for dramatic effect.

final campaign report   A write-up of a fund-raising campaign's results including statistical information and narrative summary.

fiscal federalism   The trend in the past twenty years to decentralize federal government support toward more local funding entities.

flat   In theater, a large flat piece of scenery constructed with light timber and canvas or plywood, used in a variety of ways. In music, a symbol that indicates lowering the pitch by a semitone. It is also an adjective used in music to describe a singer or musician when they are performing the note or notes slightly lower than the actual pitch.

floating capital   Funds that are currently in use; circulating capital.

fly loft   A structure anchored in the theater's walls extending the stage walls up. It is used to "fly" scenery up out of sight from the audience and also to support the grid of catwalks and technical equipment.

focus group   A group of people representative of a target audience or market to which a product or presentation is given for the purposes of getting helpful feedback.

fondu   In dance, any movement that lowers the body by bending one leg.

forestage   Part of the stage that extends beyond the proscenium toward the audience. Also called the apron.

fortissimo   A musical notation "ff" that means "very loud."

found space   A space used for performance that was not originally intended for that purpose.

fourth wall   An imaginary wall that stands between the audience and the performers on stage.

fugue   A form in music where an initial theme is established in one voice (or part).

fund-raising cycle   The typical cycle of fund-raising is planning, preparation, execution, evaluation, and planning for the next campaign.

fund-raising tripod   A fund-raising campaign is based upon purpose, leadership, and possible donors.

general-purpose grant   A grant awarded in order to support the regular work of an organization instead of a specific program.

gift analysis   A financial analysis that examines gifting for patterns that can be improved.

gift in the pipeline   A donation that has been solicited and is likely to come through.

gift leaseback   A gift of a building, equipment, or other substantial property that is then leased back to the donor at fair market value. The arrangement allows the donor to give and take a tax benefit while continuing to use the property.

gift range table or gift table   A table of gifts arranged by size, from major gifts to general gifts, in order to project how many gifts in combination are needed to achieve the campaign's final goal.

glissando A music term that means to play the notes of a chord in a quick sweep giving a harp-like effect.

grantee The person or organization receiving a grant.

grantor The person or organization making a grant.

grantsmanship The craft and ability to write successful grant proposals.

gross income All income before any deductions for expenses have been made.

growth endowment An endowment with part of its interest reinvested to offset inflation.

hanger A note at the end of a fund-raising solicitation letter from someone other than the letter-writer to add extra emphasis to the appeal.

hard money Money in the budget that is essential because it will cover operating costs.

harmony The sound of two of more notes played simultaneously or a musical term for the progression of chords in a song.

honor roll of donors A method of honoring donors, the honor roll is either published or engraved upon a plaque at regular intervals.

house organ A regular internal publication, meant only for people who employees or volunteers of an organization.

illiquid Assets that cannot be converted to cash in a timely or easy manner.

impromptu An improvised or spontaneous piece of music.

incremental budgeting Creating a budget by using a percentage of the previous year's budget.

independent sector Nonprofit organizations that are not government-sponsored nor are they associated with commercial, for-profit organizations. Also known as NGOs (non-governmental organizations) and the third sector.

indicia The mark on bulk-mailed envelopes that serves as a stamp.

initial phase The first, planning phase of a fund-raising campaign in which the case for the particular campaign is created and potential donors are identified.

insert Printed material that is enclosed with a letter or inserted into another publication.

integrated software A software program that contains another program or allows transfer of data between programs.

internal relations The working relationship between departments within one organization.

interval In music, this term refers to the pitch distance between notes.

inter vivos gift A gift that is made during a donor's lifetime (not through his or her will).

kick off The public launch of a campaign or program, usually an event.

lamp In a theater, a light bulb.

LAI The three factors that taken together identify a likely donor: Linkage, the connection to the organization; Ability, the financial capability to make a donation; and Interest, the caring and willingness to donate to an organization's cause.

Everyone Knows

Stage Directions

Stage right and stage left are your right and left as you are standing on the stage facing the audience. Upstage is toward the back of the stage away from the audience; downstage is toward the audience.

largamente A musical term that means to perform the music broadly, slowly.

legato A term indicating to play the music smoothly in a fluid and connected manner.

letter of intent A document stating the intention to give a donation, which is in some states a legally binding document.

letter shop A business that physically produces and mails direct mail advertising for an organization.

libretto The lyrics in an opera.

list broker A business that sells or rents out mailing lists for direct-mail solicitation.

list exchange An exchange between two organizations of mailing lists, usually done on a name-for-name basis and usually for a one-time use only.

load in The set up of a stage with scenery by technicians.

loaned executive A business professional who is given a leave from his or her own business to help a nonprofit with expertise for a period of time.

lock box An address, usually at a bank, where donations are mailed, opened, recorded, and deposited.

long-term liability A debt that is payable over a period of years.

lybunt A donor who contributed *last year but unfortunately not this* year.

lyrical dancing   A dance term for a poetic style of dancing with a flowing quality.

management by objective   A style of management in which measurable goals are set for an organization or a department, and then management's procedures and practices are evaluated in terms of how effective they are toward achieving those goals.

management information systems (MIS)   A computer system designed for a specific organization to help its managers conduct and record the business of the company.

managing director   In the United Kingdom, the person who directs the business affairs of a performing arts organization or department. In the United States, the chief executive officer (CEO).

market segmentation   Dividing donor or audience lists into smaller groups with similar characteristics.

matching gift   Meant to stimulate fund-raising from the public, a large gift that is given only on the condition that the organization raises an equal amount from the public within a certain period of time.

measure   The period of a musical piece that encompasses a complete cycle of the time signature.

merge-purge   The merging of two lists and deletion of duplicated names.

meter   The pattern of a music piece's rhythm of strong and weak beats.

mezzo   A musical term meaning half. Also short for "mezzo-soprano," a female vocal range between soprano and alto.

minuet   A classical music term for a dance composition played in triple (3/4) time.

moderato   A music term indicating that music be performed in a moderate tempo.

monitor service   A company that maintains fake addresses by which they help to uncover theft or misuse of a mailing list.

muses   Sister goddesses who preside over the arts and are the artist's source of inspiration.

NC (No Color)   Lighting that is white, used without color filters.

needs assessment   An evaluation of an organization or department's needs in order to determine what actions need to be taken.

new money   A gift from a new donor or a gift from an existing donor that exceeds the amount previously given.

nixie An undeliverable piece of mail returned for any reason.

nocturne From the Romantic period in music, an instrumental composition with softer dynamics than other pieces, usually intended to be performed in the evening.

notation Documenting choreography in dance. There is no universally accepted system of recording choreography and so many different systems of notation exist.

nuncupative An oral statement instead of a written document, as in a will. State law differs on the validity of nuncupative wills.

octave In music, an interval between one musical pitch and another that is either half or double its frequency.

on the book Following the prompt book throughout a performance to ensure that all of the cues are taken on time.

open the house When the audience is allowed to take their seats once a theatrical stage has been set.

operating costs All on-going costs necessary to operate an organization, including depreciation, wages, and utilities, deducted from the gross income to figure net income.

operating foundation A foundation that conducts its own research and charitable activities instead of making grants to other nonprofits.

operating statement A financial statement that compares budgets with actual income, costs, and expenditures.

organized audience movement A grassroots movement in the 1920s throughout the eastern seaboard and Great Lakes area in which local communities, eager for live theater, organized venues and subscriptions to hire performers and enable actors to tour in their area.

ostinato A short musical pattern that is repeated throughout an entire composition or a portion of a composition.

outright gift A gift from a donor who makes no restrictions upon how the donation is used.

overheads Microphones positioned over the stage or over a particular instrument to pick up sound.

pace-setting A gift in a campaign that sets the standard.

paid solicitor A person who is paid to fund-raise, often by telephone.

P and L A statement of net profit or loss for an organization over a specific period of time.

panel In printing, one section of a folded brochure.

paper the house   Giving away free tickets to a show in order to create a larger audience or to get more word-of-mouth marketing going.

partial drop   The partial mailing off of a larger, bulk mailing.

pass-through   The practice of one nonprofit receiving and disbursing funds for another organization that has not yet received its nonprofit status.

pastorale   A music term that means in a peaceful and simple style.

pattern-of-giving   The consistency of some donors to giving in the same way or in similar amounts at the same times.

payout requirement   The legal requirement that a charitable organization distribute a certain amount of charitable monies from a specific fund within a specified time.

pentatonic   In music, a scale with only five notes. It can be either major or minor.

percentage compensation   Commission.

performing arts center   Usually a multi-purpose venue, or set of venues, used to bring various performing arts to the public.

physical theater   Theatrical performance that is close to dance but more narrative in intent, it uses body "language" instead of words to convey a story.

piano   In musical notation, a direction indicating to play or sing a section of music softly, quietly or gently.

Pierian   From ancient Mount Pierus, sacred to the Muses, pierian means of or pertaining to the Muses.

pit   The sunken area in front of a stage used by the orchestra, or any area around a stage used by musicians.

pizzicato   A music term for stringed instruments that means to pluck the strings.

pop screen/shield   Thin gauze screen between a singer and a microphone or foam around the microphone to prevent "popping" of certain words (beginning with "t" or "b"), breathing sounds, or wind from distorting the song.

practical   An object that does on stage what it does in real life, such as a light switch that turns on a light when it is switched on by the actor.

precall   To call a potential donor before he or she has received a solicitation in the mail.

preliminary rating   An assessment of a potential donor as to how much he or she might be able to give.

prelude An instrumental short piece of music that precedes and sets a mood or tone as the opening introduction for the main composition.

presenter/presenting organization An organization or a department of a larger organization that creates opportunity for performing arts (dance, music, and theater) to be shared with the public. Possibly a theater, a performing arts center, or a production company, but not the troupe of performing artists themselves.

pressure label A mailing label with adhesive on the back that is peeled off its backing and applied by pressing it down on an envelope.

previews A series of public performances offered before "opening night," usually at a reduced price, that are used to fine-tune a show and spread news of the show.

price-tag The size of a donation in order to name a program or facility after the donor (usually not the actual cost of the program or facility).

private foundation Also known as a private charity, as opposed to a public charity, a private foundation does not solicit public funds but holds assets (usually from a single source, such as one person or one family) and operates using returns on investments. A private foundation makes grants to other nonprofit organizations and does not operate its own programs.

private operating foundation A private operating foundation does its own charitable programs while being funded privately with assets from a single source.

program officer At a foundation, the person who considers grant proposals and makes recommendations.

prompt book A copy of a show's script or score in which all of the technical and acting cues are noted.

props Short for "property": the various things actors use in their roles that are not part of the scenery or costumes (for example, a cup, a book, or a musical instrument).

property master The person who is in charge of supplying and keeping track of the props.

proportionate giving A gift that is balanced with the size of the project and the capacity of the donor.

proscenium arch In a traditional theater, the open space (surrounded by curtains or by ornate woodwork) through which the audience views the play. Also known as the fourth wall.

prospect   A potential donor whose affiliation (linkage), capacity for giving, and interests have been ascertained.

prospect research   Research to identify new prospects and to find further information on potential prospects.

prospect screening   Before potential donors are rated, they are sorted into more general categories of possible giving.

pro tempore   For now, for the time being, or temporarily.

psychograph   A profile of a consumer or potential donor that charts his or her lifestyle, activities, interests, consumer behavior, and personal traits in connection with financial, geographic, or demographic information.

public charity   A charitable organization funded by public, government (that is, taxpayer) money.

pull   The response rate to a direct mail advertising campaign.

Everyone

Knows

Key Unions

The following performing arts unions are affiliated with the AFL-CIO:

- American Federation of Television and Radio Artists (AFTRA)
- American Radio Association (ARA)
- Associated Actors and Artistes of America
- Actors' Equity Association (AEA)
- American Guild of Musical Artists (AGMA)
- American Guild of Variety Artists (AGVA)
- Screen Actors Guild (SAG)
- The Guild of Italian American Actors (GIAA)
- International Alliance of Theatrical Stage Employees, Moving Picture Technicians, Artists and Allied Crafts of the United States, Its Territories and Canada (IATSE)

pybunt   A donor who gave in a **p**ast **y**ear **b**ut **u**nfortunately **n**ot **t**his year. (A "past year" is not, however, the immediately preceding year, as that would make the donor a lybunt.)

qualitative research   Market research in which data about audiences, patrons, or communities are collected and analyzed to reveal behaviors and attitudes toward the organization or the organization's mission.

quantitative research   Market research in which data about audiences, patrons, or communities are collected and analyzed in a purely statistical or demographic fashion.

quarter tone   A pitch division that is half of a semitone, not often used in Western music except in jazz or experimental music.

quasi-endowment   An endowment in which the governing board members may elect to spend both the principal and the income in accordance with their judgment of the best interests of the organization.

quick-change room   A temporary, private space erected off the wings of a stage for an actor to make a quick change of costume, often with the aid of a dresser.

raked auditorium   An auditorium of seating that is progressively raised, starting from the stage and rising as it goes back.

raked stage   A stage that is slightly raised beginning downstage and rising as it goes upstage (toward the back). Historically, stages used to be raked, but now the auditorium is more likely to be raked.

reason code   A code attached to a person's name that indicates the kind of solicitation that resulted in a donation.

recency   In fund-raising, the most recent date of a donor's gift.

release   Short for a press release.

repertory   An organization of theater performers, or a theater with management and a permanent cast, in which the same cast produces a number of different shows, rehearsing and planning new shows while a current show is being performed. Each show has a set time in which to run. A repertory theater might use different actors for different shows but more often has a basic, permanent cast of actors.

reprise   A repetition later in a show of lyrics or music, often with a variation, to invoke an earlier scene.

resident company   A performance company that is said to be "resident" at a performing arts center is, at least in part and according to contract, supported by the center's administration in various ways and performs on a regular basis at the center.

resource development   Finding and creating relationships with people or organizations that are potential sources of help or funding.

response rate   The percentage of returns on a direct mail campaign or a survey.

return remit   A pre-printed business reply envelope.

reverse   A printing term that means the colors have been reversed, usually a colored or black page with white type instead of a white page with black type.

revolve   A part of the stage floor built into the floor or above the floor that turns to reveal different sets or scenery.

revolving loan   A loan that is automatically renewed when it matures.

rhapsody   A single movement work, instrumental based on folk, traditional, or popular melodies and anthems.

rondo   A musical form in which a specific section of a piece of music returns repeatedly and is interspersed with other sections.

rubato   A musical direction that means flexible in tempo, applied to notes within a musical phrase, slowing down or pausing for expressive effect.

rule of thirds   A pyramid concept in fund-raising in which the total campaign goal is divided into three parts, and the expectations is that ten donors will contribute one third, one hundred donors will contribute another third, and all of the rest of the donors will contribute the final third.

sacrificial gift   A donation that represents a real sacrifice on the part of the donor. Also known as a widow's mite.

safety curtain   A fire curtain that can be dropped on stage in case of fire to separate the stage from the audience.

salt a list   To add fake names to a list in order to determine whether or not (and how) the list is being misused or stolen. Also known as seeding a list.

sample a list   To add to a mailing list the names of people who are associated with the fund-raising campaign in order to sample the manner in which the packages are received (e.g., in a timely way, or looking clean and presentable).

save   To turn off a theater light (and thus to "save" it for later).

scrim   A thin theatrical curtain through which action can be seen if it is backlit, but which appears opaque when it is front-lit.

sectional center   A geographic location identified by the first three digits of the zip code.

seed money   An initial donation given to help kick off a fund-raising campaign.

self-mailer   A direct mail package that does not need a separate cover envelope, often a brochure that folds up, seals, and has a space for an address and postage insignia.

service organization   A nonprofit organization, such as the Association of Performing Arts Presenters or Theater Communications Group, with a mission to help other performing arts organizations.

sharp   A symbol that raises the pitch of the note by a semitone. It is also a term used to describe the intonation of a singer or musician when they are performing the note or notes slightly higher than the actual pitch of the note.

shotgun mike   A very sensitive, directional microphone that can be placed at some distance from the sound source.

shortfall   When income falls short of covering expense, the amount by which the income is less than the expense.

sightlines   Lines, often marked in the wings of the stage, along which the audience on the extreme sides of the house can see the edges of the stage. The lines help the performers stay out of sight.

sleeper   An unexpectedly important donor to a campaign; someone who was not identified as a prospect for major giving.

social capital   The part of a person's assets or income that is not used for personal expenses and is actually (or potentially) available for charitable giving.

soft money   Grant money that may not be continued.

solo break   A term in jazz that refers to an improvised cadence by a featured member of an ensemble for a section of the musical piece.

spiccato   A way of playing a violin or other stringed instrument by bouncing the bow on the string, creating a distinct staccato effect.

spotter   A member of the stage crew whose job it is to make a visual confirmation that the stage is clear and safe for scenery to be "flown" in (lowered from the ceiling).

spotting   In dance, a technique used to avoid disorientation during turns. A dancer "spots" an object or area of the room or stage and focuses on it as while turning.

staccato   A musical notation that indicates making each note short and detached. The opposite of legato.

standing committee As opposed to an-ad hoc committee, a permanent committee that works on a specific task.

stop card A card attached to a prospective donor's name with instructions to stop solicitation.

supply strategies Business strategies that focus on bringing in more revenue, sales, and production support.

swing A member of the cast who understudies several different roles or many members of the chorus. In music, a term that refers to a specific style of jazz.

SWOT analysis An organizational review that ascertains its strengths, weaknesses, opportunities, and threats.

strike the set To disassemble the set and remove all of the props.

sybunt A potential donor who has given some year but not this year.

table of gifts Based on the rule of thirds, a table that estimates the number of donors and donations needed to achieve a campaign's goal.

tabs Stage curtains.

tacet Musical notation that means to be silent.

talkback The system a sound engineer uses to talk to various people on the set. Also can refer to a headset.

tax credit An amount that is an actual credit against the amount of tax paid.

tax deductible An amount that is deductible from income, which may reduce the amount of income taxes owed.

technical assistance grant A grant specifically earmarked for an outside company to help a nonprofit with a problem that requires specialized skills for a solution.

technical rehearsal A run-through of a show in order for the technicians to rehearse lighting, sound, and so forth. A dry tech is a rehearsal without the actors; a paper tech is a run-through of the show for technicians using only the script.

tempo A musical term for the speed at which music is performed.

tenor The highest of the male voices, a vocal range that is higher than a bass but lower than an alto.

tenuto To hold a note slightly longer without changing its value.

terre-a-terre A term in dance used to describe steps in which the dancer's feet do not leave the ground.

tessitura A musical term to define the best pitch range generally identifying the most common vocal range within a piece of music.

thrust   A part of the stage that projects into the audience, so that the audience in the front is seated on both sides of it.

tickler file   A file that is created to remind oneself to do something on a particular date.

timbre   The quality of a musical tone that defines and distinguishes voices and instruments from each other.

TIN   *T*ax *i*dentification *n*umber, which is like a corporate social security number; it is used by a corporation to pay taxes.

token gift   A donation that is well below the donor's potential for giving.

top hat   A tall cylinder of metal that tops a light in order to direct the light or prevent the light from spilling into where it is not wanted.

transom   From times past, a little hinged window in the top of a door where today's spy hole might be. An over the transom donation is an unexpected gift from a donor who was not previously identified.

transparency   The quality in an organization in which its activities, finances, deals, to name a few, are readily apparent to the public eye. The quality of keeping little hidden.

travesti   A term in dance that refers to when a female dancer is dancing a male role in a man's costume or when a male dancer is dancing a female role in a woman's costume.

tremelo   A rapid repetition of the same note.

trim size   In printing, the size of a brochure or publication after it has been printed and trimmed.

tripod of giving   Three traditional ways in which a donor may give (1) contributing to an annual fund (2) contributing to a capital fund, or (3) contributing to or creating an endowment.

troupe   A company of performers.

turnout   In dance, a stance that is the foundation of ballet, in which the legs are rotated outward from the hips so that the knees and feet point in opposite directions.

una corda   In piano music, this term refers to producing the sound of a note in such a way that the hammer is striking only one string.

unearned income   Income that is not the result of sales or services provided, such as philanthropic gifts or interest income.

unified credit   A lifetime tax credit, in an amount determined by the federal government (currently $345,800) that is applied against taxes owed on a gift or bequest. The tax on the gift is determined, and then the credit it applied against the tax. Currently, $1,000,000 can be gifted without tax liability if someone's entire lifetime gift tax credit is used.

unisono In music, a term that means musicians playing exactly the same note together at the same time, in unison.

upgrade In fund-raising, an effort to increase a donor's level of giving.

upstage The part of the stage that is toward the back, away from the audience. To upstage is to draw attention away from the main action or actor.

variable annuity An annuity that pays out a variable income based upon the value of the investment portfolio.

vibrato A rapidly repeated slight alteration in the pitch of a note used to give a richer sound.

virtuoso A musician of exceptional artistry who performs with outstanding technique.

visual cue A technical cue that is taken from the action on the stage rather than from a stage manager.

vocal score A musical score for an opera composition or a vocal or choral composition with orchestra where the vocal parts are written out.

volee de In dance, a term that means "in flight" and indicates that a specific step is to be done with a soaring or flying movement.

walk-on In a show, a small part in which the actor has no lines.

wallet envelope An envelope with a detachable flap that can be printed with additional information about a campaign.

waltz A dance in 3/4 time.

wash A single lighting color that "washes" across the whole stage.

white mail A donation that arrives in the donor's own envelope instead of the organization's preprinted return envelope.

wing flats Flats that hide actors in the wings (the sides of the stage that are just out of the audience's view).

working leg A term in dance for the leg that is executing a given movement while the weight of the body is on the other leg.

year-end gift A donation made within the last two months of the year, often with a tax benefit in mind.

Chapter 6

Resources

One of the wonderful things about the performing arts is the sense of camaraderie amongst its practitioners. Whether it is because artists and arts managers feel like they live in a beleaguered nation or simply due to their expansive love of the art, performing arts practitioners love to help others in this field. Thus, resources abound. From associations and organizations to help artists and performers to agencies created to help management and presenters; from educational institutions hosting workshops to professional organizations hosting conferences; from print publications focused on what is new to online publications focused on where to go next—if you look you will probably find resources to help grow your professional career and personal skills, no matter what shoes you find yourself trying to fill.

Associations and Organizations

American Council on Gift Annuities is an organization that promotes responsible philanthropy by recommending annuity rates, and with training and advocacy. The Council's site includes both a Donor's Corner and a Sponsor's Forum. (http://www.acga-web.org)

General Arts Organizations

Americans for the Arts is a national nonprofit organization serving local communities in advancing all forms of the arts. The
organization cultivates specialized programs and services that
foster an environment to create opportunities in which the arts
can thrive. It provides arts industry research, information, and
development opportunities for community arts leaders, and generates public and private sector resources for the arts and arts
education. (http://www.americansforthearts.org)

Arts Advise is a consulting network that offers practical guidance
to the arts community and nonprofit organizations. Arts Advise
consultants help provide evaluation and direction in long range
planning, board development, organizational structure, staffing, programs, fund-raising, marketing and publicity, and earned
income generation. (http://www.artsadvise.net)

Arts in Crisis is a Kennedy Center initiative providing free consulting and emergency planning assistance to struggling nonprofit
501(c)(3) arts organizations. The program offers free counsel in
fund-raising, budgeting, marketing, and other areas of arts management that may be affected by difficult economic times. (http://
www.artsincrisis.org)

Arts and Business Council of Americans for the Arts builds
private sector support for the arts through national programs
encouraging partnerships between the arts and business. Programs include Business Volunteers for the Arts, National Arts
Forum Series, Arts Based Corporate Training, and National Arts
Marketing Project. (http://www.artsusa.org)

Arts Consulting Group is a national firm that provides fund-raising and marketing for consulting, program and facilities planning, and organizational development services for the arts and
culture industry. They also provide a monthly e-newsletter, "Arts
Insights". (http://www.artsconsulting.com)

Arts Management Network is an international network for arts
and business providing resources, information on arts management, arts-related conferences, associations, books, courses, Web
sites, articles, and organizations. (http://www.artsmanagement
.net)

Association of Performing Arts Presenters represents both the
nonprofit and for-profit sectors of the performing arts industry.
Its members encompass national and international arts presenters,

On the Cutting Edge

The Technological Revolution

Television did not kill radio, the recording industry did not kill symphony orchestras, and movies did not kill theater—but technology does change everything. As Tyler Cowen (a writer on cultural economics) points out, today's technology keeps revolutionizing the performing arts and the entertainment business—indeed, the economy and culture itself. One basic fact, however, remains a constant anchor for performing arts managers: People like to connect. If what people seek is immediacy and interaction with other people, nothing can provide that better than physically being at a live performance. What popular technologies have today that live performances do not is audience participation: ways in which audiences can—without taking any risks themselves—become a part of the action.

How will technology continue to be integrated into the performing arts? That remains to be created by the performing arts managers of the future. Perhaps it means something more immediate in an audience's participation in live performance, some combination of technology and live performance that could create an interface, a virtual feedback into the real. Or perhaps the answer is some kind of group experience, some facilitated interaction of the audience within itself that creates new bonds, new friendships, and a new sense of community.

ranging from large performing arts centers and academic institutions to community organizations, festivals, artists, and artist managers. APAP is made up of an expansive and diverse performing arts membership. The association hosts a Web site that is an online resource for grants, networking, news, training, and events, and it produces an annual conference to provide exhibits, meetings, workshops, performance showcases, and networking opportunities for arts presenters, artists, and arts managers. (http://www.artspresenters.org)

Association of Arts Administration Educators is an international organization representing college and university graduate and undergraduate programs in arts administration. AAAE advocates formal training for arts administrators in the management of arts organizations and encourages members to publish and present research for the arts management administration community to help provide information about arts management to both the academic and professional fields. (http://www.artsadministration.org)

Association of Fund-Raising Professionals fosters development and growth of fund-raising professionals for nonprofit organizations by providing information, publications, advocacy, resources, and sets high ethical standards in the fund-raising profession. (http://www.afpnet.org)

BBB Wise Giving Alliance merges the U.S. Better Business Bureau with the National Charities Information Bureau and gives donors solid advice about national charities. It produces in-depth reports on charities and publishes the Wise Giving Guide. Nonprofits that meet the criteria can participate in the Alliance's National Charity Seal program. (http://www.bbb.org/us/wise-giving)

BoardSource is a nonprofit organization dedicated to helping other nonprofits develop effective board members. BoardSource offers workshops, training, membership, consulting, publications, and an annual conference. (http://www.boardsource.org)

Broadway League is the national trade association for the Broadway industry. Members include theater owners, producers, presenters, and general managers in North American Cities as well as suppliers of goods and services to the commercial theater industry. The League is a full-service trade association dedicated to fostering interest in Broadway theater and serving the needs of theatrical producers in New York and of national touring shows, as well as presenters of touring productions in cities throughout North America. The League sponsors an annual event "Broadway on Broadway" to bring together stars and performances from current and upcoming Broadway productions. (http://www.broadwayleague.com)

Chorus America is a nonprofit organization designed to provide training, advocacy, information, networking, news, and leadership development to strengthen choral groups and choral organizations across the country. Programs include Singer Network, EVoice, Chorus Management Institute, and the annual Chorus America Conference. (http://www.chorusamerica.org)

The Commercial Theater Institute is a project of Theater Development Fund and the Broadway League. Dedicated to training the next generation of commercial theater producers, CTI provides resources, programs, seminars and guidance to individuals and theater professionals with information about various aspects of creating commercial productions for the stage. (http://www.commercialtheaterinstitute.com)

Dance USA is a national organization providing services to the professional dance field. Its membership represents a broad cross section of dance companies, as well as presenting organizations and related organizations. Member services include public communications, advocacy, research, information, and branch offices. (http://www.danceusa.org)

Folk Alliance International serves over 2,000 members worldwide and hosts an annual conference for folk music and dance that is one of the five largest music conferences in North America. The Folk Alliance community encourages membership from both the non-profit and for-profit fields of folk music including record companies, publishers, arts presenters, agents, managers, music support services, manufacturers, musicians, performers, songwriters, and other artists that work in the folk music world. Folk Alliance has six regional affiliates that provide the grass roots efforts in their respective markets. (http://www.folkalliance.org)

Fractured Atlas is a nonprofit organization serving the national community of artists and arts organizations through providing programs, services, education, healthcare, resources, funding, and fiscal sponsorship. The goal of Fractured Atlas is to foster an environment that nurtures the independent spirit in artists, arts organizations, and communities. The organization represents a community of artists from every discipline and provides support to underrepresented talents in all forms of the performing arts. (http://www.fracturedatlas.org)

International Society for the Performing Arts is a nonprofit organization of performing arts professionals from more than 50 countries, working to strengthen the arts through programs, networking, and conferences to cultivate a deeper global exchange. Members include presenting organizations, independent artists, performing arts organizations, artist managers, cultural policy groups, foundations, and consultants. (http://www.ispa.org)

League of American Orchestras is an advocate for a diverse membership of orchestras of all sizes linking a national network of instrumentalists, conductors, managers, volunteers, staff, board members, and business partners in the orchestra field, providing advocacy, information, educational programs, and leadership opportunities. (http://www.americanorchestras.org)

National Alliance for Musical Theater is a national service organization for musical theater. Members include theaters, presenting organizations, universities, and producers. NAMT promotes the creation, development, production, and presentation of new and classic musicals. It also provides a forum for resources and information specific to musical theater through communications, networking, and programming. (http://www.namt.org)

National Arts Strategies is an organization providing executive education for arts and culture organizations through seminars, networking, publications, and programs like Business of Arts and Culture (tm) and The NAS Exchange (tm). (http://www.artstrategies .org)

National Performance Network provides support, resources, and creative guidance for the independent artist community. It consists of a network of adventurous and dedicated partner-member presenters working with a centralized source of national funds for the presentation of work and extended artists' residencies in communities. The network is comprised of 55 NPN partners, in 43 cities across the United States with the mission of facilitating partnerships, subsidizing artists' residencies, and nurturing an imaginative, progressive leadership with both artists and presenters. (http://www.npnweb.org)

North American Performing Arts Managers and Agents is a nonprofit association promoting the professionalism and mutual advancement of performing arts managers, agents, artist managers, self-managed artists, business vendors and presenters in the live performing arts. NAPAMA acts a resource for its members by providing education; publications; workshops; forums for regional, national, international meetings; and research and development for sound business practices. (http://www.napama.org)

Opera America is a service organization in North America promoting the creation, development, and presentation of opera. Membership includes professional opera and semi-professional companies, international affiliated opera companies, businesses, educational institutions, libraries, foundations, guilds, and opera artists such as singers and composers. The organization provides artistic services that help artists and companies in the following ways: increasing the creativity and excellence of opera productions; offering opera company services that address the needs of

Professional
Ethics

Common Lessons for Ethical Dilemmas

After finishing graduate school and putting in two years on the job as executive assistant to the director of corporate support at a huge performing arts festival in Maine, you were incredibly exited to land the position of development director for a small performing arts center in Phoenix, Arizona. One of the first projects you need to tackle is finding money to finish the amphitheater renovation. The amphitheater's stage and seating are brand-new and state of the art. The problem is the electrical wiring–including stage lighting, safety lighting, and parking lot lighting. The newly installed electrical systems mysteriously burned out a few weeks before you started. The price for installing a new system is $275,000. The college's fiscal year is drawing to a close, budgets have been spent, and there is only $175,000 in reserve that can be used for the project. You have to find another $100,000. Fast.

Your first move is to meet with the Pinyon Center's board of directors. Everyone on the board is local enough to get together on short notice. President McClure, chairman of the board, also attends the meeting. You see that he is holed up with one board member, Marshall Armstrong, the CEO of a local chain

staff, trustees, and volunteers; and providing educational services in the community that increase opera appreciation. (http://www.operaamerica.org)

Performing Arts Alliance is a national network of professional, nonprofit performing arts and presenting fields and an advocate for arts organizations, artists, and their publics before the U.S. Congress and key policy makers. Through legislative and grassroots action, the Performing Arts Alliance advocates for national policies that recognize and enhance the arts in America. (http://www.theperformingartsalliance.org)

Theater Communications Group is a nonprofit organization serving theater communities on the local, national and international level. TCG seeks to increase efficiency of member theaters, of restaurants. When you discuss the meeting afterwards with McClure, he announces the whole problem has been solved. Marshall Armstrong has already worked out a deal with Tempe, Arizona contractor P & G Electric. They will do the whole job for $175,000! Since the new fiscal year begins in only three weeks, President McClure feels it is okay to use up the center's cash reserve on this great deal. Instantly, your surprise turns to dread, because you have done your homework before this meeting (that is, learning all you can about each board member) and you know Marshall Armstrong is part owner of P & G Electric.

The most important thing to remember in this or any other ethical dilemma is not to act rashly. Seek the counsel of your mentor. Do your homework and know your company and co-workers. Begin your dealings with others with respect and appreciation. Consider whether private conversation would be better than public discussion. Try to turn your criticisms into suggestions for improvement; in this situation, it may mean talking personally with Marshall Armstrong, telling him delicately that even the *appearance* of a conflict of interest will damage the center as well as himself. Always ask before you accuse. Finally, and most importantly, make decisions based upon what you personally believe is right.

cultivate artistry and achievements of the field, and promote a greater appreciation for theater through programs, conferences, publications, networking, and resources. Among its many services, TCG awards grants to artistic programs for theaters and theater artists; offers career development programs for artists; provides professional development opportunities for theater leaders through conferences and forums; extends advocacy through guides and lobbying efforts; and provides member theaters with timely alerts about legislative developments. TCG provides information through its magazine, American Theater, and the ARTSEARCH employment bulletin. It also publishes plays, translations, theater reference books, and dramatic literature. (http://www.tcg.org)

Theater Intern Group offers social and professional development opportunities for students and individuals who are beginning a career in the theater industry. The group provides professional networking opportunities where interns can build contacts for their career, volunteer openings, job opportunities, and monthly panel discussions with theater professionals focusing on current for-profit theater topics such as theater and the Internet, theatrical press and publicity, marketing and advertising, general management, and agents. TIG also provides tickets to Broadway and off-Broadway shows so that members can see new works for free. (http://theaterinterngroup.org)

Western Arts Alliance is a membership organization of touring and performing arts professionals working in promoting and presenting performing arts in all fields. (http://www.westarts.org)

Books and Periodicals

Books

There are two main types of books. Craft books help your skills. Professional titles address strategy.

Trade

Arts Marketing Insights: The Dynamics of Building and Retaining Performing Arts Audiences. By Joanne Scheff Bernstein and Philip Kotler (Jossey-Bass, 2006). A resource for arts professionals that offers a fresh look at the challenges, methodologies, and opportunities for arts organizations to build audiences and connect with patrons, to improve financial health, and to develop marketing campaigns.

Arts Management. By Derrick Chong (Routledge, 2002). The artistic, managerial and social responsibilities of arts management is explored in this work that educates both arts managers and students, delving into the challenges and conditions of arts organizations in association with critical issues in management.

History of the Theatre, Vol. 1. By Arthur Hornblow (J.B. Lippencott, 1919). Great stories of theater history from an older perspective. (http://www.theatrehistory.com/american/hornblow04.html)

Human Resource Policies and Procedures for Nonprofit Organizations. By Carol L. Barbeito (Wiley, 2006). Practical information and tools for developing effective human resource management for nonprofit organizations are covered in this book that provides a framework for developing management systems, policies and procedures applicable for nonprofit organizations of all types.

Management and the Arts. By William J. Byrnes (Focal Press, 1992). A comprehensive overview of the field of arts management, now in its third edition.

Managing Creativity: The Dynamics of Work and Organization. By Howard Davis and Richard Scase (Open University Press, 2000). Howard Davis, a professor of social theory and institutions, and Richard Scase, a professor of organizational behavior, explore the creative industries as a growing economic and cultural force and investigate organizational dynamics of incorporating structures that best utilize the talents of creative employees.

Performing Arts: The Economic Dilemma. By William J. Baumol and William G. Bowen (Ashgate Publishing, 1993). A classic study that offers an extensive analysis of the primary economic dynamics and problems in the performing arts.

Standing Room Only: Strategies for Marketing the Performing Arts. By Joanne Scheff Bernstein and Philip Kotler (Harvard Business School Press, 1997). An in-depth look at marketing, marketing concepts, and the performing arts market for nonprofit performing arts organizations. This study discusses the challenges of waning government support and increased competition.

The Art of the Turnaround: Creating and Maintaining Healthy Arts Organizations. By Michael M. Kaiser (Brandeis University Press, 2008). Practical advice for art organizations in crisis supported by practical case studies with guidance for fixing struggling arts organizations by Michael M. Kaiser, President and CEO of the John F. Kennedy Center for the Performing Arts.

The Capacity of Performing Arts Presenting Organizations. By Mark A. Hager and Thomas H. Pollak (The Urban Institute, 2002). An influential study reporting on the ability of organizations to present performance and sustain themselves financially. (http://www.urban.org/publications/410604.html)

The Economics of Art and Culture. By James Heilbrun and Charles Gray (Cambridge University Press, 2001). The economics of the fine arts and performing arts is explored in this work that also covers public policy toward the arts at federal, state, and local levels in the United States.

Theatre Management in America. By Stephen Langley (Drama Book Publishers, 1995). A comprehensive book that covers all aspects of theatrical management for nonprofit arts organizations and commercial theater.

Yours For The Asking: An Independent Guide to Fund-Raising and Management. By Reynold Levy (Wiley, 2008). Balancing practical advice with career experience in both business and philanthropy, this is a compact and instructive book that provides insight to staff members, board members, volunteers, and management of nonprofit organizations.

Professional

Arts and Culture in the Metropolis: Strategies for Sustainability. By Kevin McCarthy, Elizabeth Heneghan Ondaatje, and Jennifer Novak (RAND, 2007). A major study on maintaining financial health in the modern metropolis.

Booking and Tour Management for the Performing Arts. By Rena Shagan (Allworth Press, 2001). Third edition of Shagan's classic reference book on arts management for touring performing groups and individual artists.

Changing the Performance: A Companion Guide to Arts, Business and Civic Relations. By Julia Rowntree (Routledge, 2006). Based on the writer's experiences creating business sponsorship campaigns with London arts organizations, Rowntree explores the arts and business and discusses how the two affect each other.

How to Run a Theater: A Witty, Practical and Fun Guide to Arts Management. By Jim Volz (Back Stage Books, 2004). A resource for those who work in arts management at all levels, this humorous and insightful guide to arts management provides a wide range of helpful information on fund-raising, building audiences, financial management, marketing, and cultivating strong productive relationships with boards, volunteers, and communities.

Innovation, Dissemination, and Leadership in a Changing Arts Landscape. By Suzanne Sato (Doris Duke Charitable Foundation, 2007). While this study was written for the Doris Duke Foundation in order to review its funding strategy, the study provides an excellent overview of the state of the industry.

Organizational Culture and Leadership. By Edgar H. Schein (Jossey Bass, 1985). A pioneer in the field, Schein discusses how to foster growth and shape the culture of an organization in any stage of development, moving it towards practicing greater effectiveness.

Performing Arts Management: A Handbook of Professional Practices. By Tobie S. Stein and Jessica Bathurst (Allworth Press, 2008). In this thorough overview of performing arts management, managers of leading nonprofit organizations and commercial venues explore strategies that work in all areas of performing arts management.

State Arts Policy: Trends and Future Prospects. By Julia Lowell (Rand, 2008). A look at recent changes in funding policies helps clarify the trends for performing arts organizations.

The Arts at a New Frontier: The National Endowment for the Arts. By Fannie Taylor and Anthony L. Barresi (Springer, 1984). A classic overview from the modern era.

The Art of Governance: Boards in the Performing Arts. By Nancy Roche and Jaan W. Whitehead (eds.) (Theatre Communications Group, 2005). The fiscal stability of arts organizations is the foundation upon which creative works are presented. This book is a guide for trustees in the performing arts and for the artists, managers, and community leaders working with arts organizations. It discusses various case studies of institutions and national policies of the performing arts while also exploring board development, planning, finance, and fund-raising.

The 11 Questions Every Donor Asks and the Answers All Donors Crave. By Harvey McKinnon (Emerson and Church, 2008). In this engaging and insightful book, eleven core questions are identified as key in the art of fund-raising and the cornerstone of communication to inspire generous donations.

The Fund-Raising Habits of Supremely Successful Boards. By Jerold Panas (Emerson and Church, 2006). A guide for organizations and their board members, this book discusses how to cultivate the most effective business habits for resource development—whether managing, securing, or strengthening the financial stability of a nonprofit organization.

The Performing Arts in a New Era. By Kevin McCarthy, Arthur Brooks, Julia Lowell, and Laura Zakaras (RAND, 2001). An influential study that helped define the state of the industry at the turn of the century.

The Performing Arts: Problems and Prospects. By the Rockefeller Brothers Fund (McGraw-Hill, 1965). This Rockefeller Panel Report is a classic study on the future of theater, music, dance, art, and performing arts organizations in America

Periodicals

American Theatre Magazine is a publication of the Theatre Communications Group with a focus on theater issues, theater works, and issues concerning theater artists, managers, and organizations nationwide. (http://www.tcg.org/publications)

Dance Magazine is an award winning magazine for performing, audiences, and managers in the multi-faceted field of dance. The magazine publishes resource listings, interviews, and feature stories on dancers, dance productions, and organizations. (http://www.dancemagazine.com)

International Arts Manager Magazine is a resource for professional arts managers in the performing arts worldwide. (http://www.impromptupublishing.com/gig.html)

Journal of Arts Management, Law and Society is a resource for the field of performing, visual, and media arts, addressing issues in arts policy, management, law, and governance. (http://www.heldref.org/pubs/jamls/about.html)

Symphony Magazine is the League of Orchestra's bimonthly magazine. Published both in hard copy and online, it features articles on issues relevant to musicians, orchestra members, arts managers, board members, professional staff, patrons, volunteers, and audiences of orchestra across the country. (http://www.americanorchestras.org/symphony_magazine/symphony_magazine.html)

The Voice is a quarterly magazine of Chorus America, available both as a hard copy subscription or online called E-Voice. The magazine features in-depth interviews and profiles, chorus news and activities, commentary, board leadership strategies, fundraising and marketing techniques, announcements, ads, and other arts-related information. (http://www.chorusamerica.org/publications.cfm)

Web Sites

American Arts Alliance sponsors a Web site providing advocacy tools, arts education, and legislation related to art organizations. (http://www.americanartsalliance.org)

Americans for the Arts provides an online library with an extensive listing of resources on arts management, arts education and nonprofit arts organizations through their Public Awareness Campaign page. (http://www.americansforthearts.org/public_awareness)

"American Theatre History" is a great review of theater history by Arthur L. Dirks, Professor of Theater, Bridgewater State College. (http://webhost.bridgew.edu/adirks/ald/courses/hist/hist_Amer .htm)

Arts Consulting Group hosts an online archive of articles in the arts management field. (http://www.artsconsulting.com/artsinsights)

Artsjournal.com provides new sources of arts management information and job listings, and is home to Andrew Taylor's popular blog "The Artful Manager." (http://www.artsjournal.com)

Arts Management Network posts current articles on topics related to arts management, as well as updated links to resources and arts management information. (http://artsmanagement.net)

Best
Practice

Scholarly Articles

The following scholarly articles, some available online, are well worth seeking out to get a detailed view various areas of the performing arts industry.

- **"The Ford Era"** presents a glimpse into performing arts history, helping to put the modern era of corporate grant-making into perspective. Written by John Kreidler and available at (http://www.inmotionmanagine.com/lost2.html)

- **"How to Save the Performing Arts"** by Michael M. Kaiser gives his forumula for staying strong in a difficult economy. *The Washington Post*, December 29, 2002.

- **"Why Everything Has Change: The Recent Revolution in Cultural Economics"** by Tyler Cowen presents a comprehensive, clear view of contemporary funding in the performing arts. *Journal of Cultural Economics* v.32, 2008.

- **"Staging an Ancient Greek Play"** written by Walter Englert, Omar and Althea Hoskins Professor of Classical Studies at Reed College, is a wonderful description of theater history. (http://academic.reed .edu/humanities/110tech/staging.html)

ArtsManager.org is an online resource community for arts managers and arts organizations to network, share their expertise, and develop new strategies. The site features discussion, news, and a blog from Kennedy Center president Michael M. Kaiser. (http://artsmanagerfba.artsmanager.org/KCBlogs/default.aspx)

Arts Opportunities.org is a service provided by the Center for Arts Management and Technology that shares listing information for jobs, internships, mentoring, training programs, and conferences in the arts field. (http://www.artsopportunities.org)

Compasspoint.org provides services to nonprofit organizations, including an online newsletter called "Board Café" and the Web resource "Nonprofit Genie," both of which offer news and practical advice from leading organizational management experts on a range of topics. (http://www.compasspoint.org)

Energizeinc.com provides information and news through its online management library. (http://www.energizeinc.com/art.html)

Guidestar.org is an online directory and comprehensive resource database of nonprofit organizations. The Web site's in-depth profiles are provided by the organizations themselves for outreach and online access by potential donors. (http://www.guidestar.org)

Management Assistance Program for Nonprofits sponsors a Web site that provides "The Complete Tool Kit for Boards," an extensive library of online tools for nonprofit corporations, including board manuals, forms, fact sheets, and sample policies. (http://www.managementhelp.org/boards/boards.htm)

"Managing the Road" is another fine review of theater history by Arthur L. Dirks. (http://webhost.bridgew.edu/adirks/ald/courses/hist/hist_econ.htm)

National Center for Nonprofit Boards provides tools and information to nonprofit organizations and their board members through an online resource called Board Source. (http://www.boardsource.org)

Performing Arts Alliance hosts a Web site that advocates for and reports on legislative and grassroots action on policies that affect nonprofit arts organizations. (http://www.theperformingartsalliance.org)

Volunteermatch.org is an online resource for partnering volunteers with nonprofit organizations. The Web site also provides advice for volunteer managers, tools for managing volunteer hours, and a monthly newsletter. (http://www.volunteermatch.org)

Educational Institutions

Center for Arts Management and Technology at Carnegie Melon is an applied research center with programs that connect the artistic community with innovative technology solutions and services that improve efficiency, expand outreach, and increase effectiveness. The Center offers professional development workshops and seminars. (http://camt.artsnet.org)

DePaul University offers a performing arts management program, culminating in a bachelor of music degree with a concentration in performing arts management and a minor in business administration. (http://www.depaul.edu/academics/undergraduate/majors/manageperformarts.asp)

Emerging Leadership Institute is an annual seminar program of the Association of Performing Arts Presenters. (http://www.artspresenters.org/services)

Emerson College has a performing arts administration certificate program, a non-degree course of study available to managers of performing arts and nonprofit cultural organizations. (http://www.emerson.edu/ce/programs/certificate/Performing-Arts-Admin.cfm)

Institute for the Management of Creative Enterprises is a joint program of Carnegie Mellon University's College of Fine Arts and the Heinz College. Programs include master of arts management at the Center of Arts Management and Technology, and master of entertainment industry management at the Arts and Culture Observatory. (http://www.artsnet.org)

Kennedy Center Arts Management Programs are available to individuals and organizations. The programs include International Cultural Mentoring Program, International Arts Management Training Program, a variety of internship programs, the Fellowship Program, and the International Fellowship Program. (http://www.kennedy-center.org/education/artsmanagement)

New York University offers the Steinhardt Performing Arts Administration Summer Study, an international seminar for graduate students, alumni of arts administration programs and arts management professionals. Students explore current cultural and social issues affecting international arts practices and gain insights into managing arts organizations around the world. (http://steinhardt.nyu.edu/music/artsadmin/programs/summer)

University of Massachusetts Amherst Arts Management Certificate Program is an online distance learning program for arts
managers and students. The Fundamentals of Arts Management
Online is a five-part series of online courses covering planning,
board development, fund raising, marketing, and arts programming.   (http://www.elearners.com/college/university-of-
massachusetts-online)

Yale University has a theater management program through the
School of Drama. Though focused primarily on theater organizations, it incorporates training relevant to other performing arts
and nonprofit organizations. (http://www.yale.edu/drama)

Index

of development
    communications, 55
  great, 26
  job description of, 45, 49
  need for, 12
  training of, 13-16
managerial assistant, 51
Managing Creativity: The Dynamics of Work and Organization (Davis and Scase), 127
managing director, 60, 107
"Managing the Road" (Dirks), 132
Mapplethorpe, Robert, 22
marketing and promotions
    assistant, 69
marketing/public relations, 63, 66-70
market segmentation, 107
matching gift, 107
"matching grants," 12, 18
"Mat Medley." *See* Aston, Anthony
Maywood, Augusta, 6
McCarthy, Kevin, 23, 128, 129
McKinnon, Harvey, 129
measure, 107
Mellon Foundation, 11
mentors, 92
    caution in choosing, 90
    establishing relationships
        with, 89-90
    finding, 83-84, 87
    friendships with, 83
    giving back to, 90
    how-to, 84-85
    identifying, 84-85, 88
    importance of, viii, 87
    needs of, 89
    number of, 82
    personal, 85-88
    timing with, 80, 89
    types of, 84
    what are, 83
Merce Cunningham Dance
    Company, 14-15, 44
merge-purge, 107

meter, 107
mezzo, 107
minuet, 107
moderato, 107
monitor service, 107
Mount Pieria, 6
muses, 6, 107
music, xiv
    classical, 29-31
    for-profit, 31, 34-36
    opera, 29-30
musical theater, pop-culture
    versions, 28-29

N

NAMT. *See* National Alliance for
    Musical Theater
NAPAMA. *See* North American
    Performing Arts Managers and
    Agents
NASSA. *See* National Assembly of
    State Arts Agencies
National Alliance for Musical
    Theater (NAMT), 123
National Arts and Cultural
    Development Act (1964), 10, 18
National Arts Strategies, 123
National Assembly of State Arts
    Agencies (NASSA), 10
National Association of Concert
    Managers, 12
National Center for Nonprofit
    Boards, 132
National Council for the Arts, 10,
    18
National Cultural Center, 10
National Endowment for the Arts
    (NEA), 14
    establishment of, 10, 12, 15,
        18
    as service organization, 43
National Foundation on the Arts
    and Humanities Act (1965), 10
National Performance Network
    (NPN), 123